FALLEN FROM THE NEST

D1512312

Clotilde Noël

MARIAN PRESS
STOCKBRIDGE MA 01263
PRO CHRISTO ET ECCLESIA

2021

DEDICATION

For you, Nicolas, without whom this beautiful story
would be impossible. Thanks.
How lucky to experience such powerful dreams together!

For you, of course, Côme, Baudouin, Tiphaine,
Marin, Philippine, Brune, and Marie.

And for all my godchildren, who are so important to me:
Jeanne, Tancrède, Clarisse, Marie-Hermine, Tiphaine,
Augustine, Eudes, and Hortense.

"*I really must put up with two or three caterpillars
if I want to become acquainted with butterflies.
It seems that they are so beautiful.*"
— Antoine de Saint-Exupéry

"*You cannot caress when your hands are closed.*"
— Jean-Jacques Goldman

CONTENTS

PUBLISHER'S NOTE

Fallen from the Nest by Clotilde Noël is a French mother's heartfelt memoir of her family's experience of the adoption process, unveiling their journey from when she and her husband, Nicolas, made the decision to adopt a child with special needs to when the adoption finally became official — a journey of six years.

During the two-year adoption process, Clotilde wrote letters to the child who would eventually become a part of their large, loving family. In the letters, she recorded her family's loving anticipation of welcoming the child; aspects of their everyday lives, including the death of a beloved aunt; and their challenges with the French authorities along the way. In translating these beautiful reflections from the original French into English, we have tried to remain true to Ms. Noël's voice and messages, while also making her meaning clear to an English-reading audience.

The preface was written by Mr. Tim Guénard and his wife, Martine, who are well-acquainted with the French authorities whom the Noëls dealt with. Tim was abandoned and abused as a child, and was moved from foster home to foster home throughout his young life. In an excerpt from his book *Stronger than Hate*, he states "For years I lived off the flame of revenge. While in my prison of hate, I was visited by people filled with love; within my heart they brought me to my knees. I owe my life to the broken, distraught, [disabled] and 'abnormal' people whom our society has rejected. I also learned from them a tremendous lesson about love." Tim and Martine now assist distressed people in their home near Lourdes, France.

We were overjoyed to learn in 2021 that Pope Francis had recognized the heroic virtues of Dr. Jerome Lejeune, who discovered the cause of Down syndrome and dedicated his life to providing care and advocating for the medically vulnerable. Dr. Lejeune, whose cause for canonization was opened in 2007, has now been raised to the status of "Venerable."

The Jerome Lejeune Foundation carries on his work and is one of the largest funders of research, care, and advocacy for these medically vulnerable populations. In fact, little Marie was helped by the Foundation. The afterword in this book is written by Dr. Aimé Ravel, a pediatrician qualified in medical genetics and consulting manager of the Jérôme Lejeune Institute in France.

It is our hope that this moving story about the power of pure love will touch you as deeply as it has touched us.

— Marian Press

PREFACE

We have just finished reading your testimony, dear Clotilde. We have even read the summary to be sure not to have missed anything from your precious work — to be certain that there were no pearls left in the recesses of the document. We have eagerly devoured your words with a heart that receives abundance and does not want to miss a thing.

While reading it, I returned to my mother's and grandmother's womb. You described your impressions and feelings so well that you opened a door on mine. Thanks to you, every mother will be able to make another journey into her adoptions or births.

It is through your feelings and wifely look that you had your child discover her father's love. You did not fall into the pitfall of speaking in her name. You watched her up until the day when you saw that her father's heart was forever touched.

You made sure to give all of your children their place in anticipation of the mystery of another life. They were not an amorphous group of siblings, but six distinct little beings who were reaching out toward the seventh one, each in their own way.

There were eight hearts and sixteen arms ready to receive Marie. They would make up her new nest. They were a family — not a perfect model that could not be surpassed by anything. They were a family motivated by love, life's surprises, and the desire for everyone's growth and respect.

Thank you, Clotilde, for linking Marie's life to the death — new life — of your dear aunt. It is the same MYSTERY that unites all our lives. You cannot not "prove" it. How does one prove a mystery? You make us touch it with our fingers. You speak so well of the only golden thread that allows us to touch this mystery, which is LOVE.

However, like you, we have met some people who have lost track of where their lives are going due to the fact that they no longer believe in love at all. They are suspicious that the one who loves for love's sake is hiding other motivations, earning more money, etc. We have been astonished and have had a hard time thinking that they do not believe in love. To want to adopt a "normal" child is acceptable, but it is fishy to want to adopt a disabled child! And if you have already encountered a disability in your life — but no, never. This is even more fishy! Why is Marie for you? Why are you for Marie?

You often brought us into the labyrinth of a kind of frightening trial that we thought we would never get out of. We could not speak. Nonetheless, you did not linger in criticism and complaining. Without wasting time, you fought with the weapons of your truth and with the support of professionals who are worthy of their position. These two years were endless for you. Some will have a hard time believing it. They will think, "This is too outrageous. Social workers cannot be so inhuman. This is exaggerated!" But we do not question any of your words. They are the truth.

Thank you, Clotilde, for speaking to us about love, not in a sappy way, but as an extravagance, a time that never ends, a strength that unites us, and an achievement! Throughout these pages, we have often wondered how you have been able to continue. You have shown us love as a strength that "bears all things, believes all things, hopes all things, endures all things," and that "never ends," as St. Paul tell us (see 1 Cor 13:7-8).

We are struck by your equilibrium. Your sense of reason remained in this crazy journey toward Marie — as you accommodated everyone, prepared the ground for Marie's arrival as well as possible, recognized the advantage of time delays, and were eager for advice. You were free in your resolve, with an equal measure of wisdom and mirth.

Your story does not need a preface. But we thank our dear nephews for the immense gift that they gave us to think of us in the preface of your letter and book, according to the custom. They knew that our stories send signs of gratitude to each other. Incidentally, it is a letter that we are writing to you today.

My [Martine's] adolescence was brightened by two cousins who have a severe physical disability. They lit up my whole life and prepared me for 40 years of happiness working at the OCH (Office Chrétien des Personnes Handicapées — Christian Office for Disabled Persons), which connected me to hundreds of families and guides. My life with them was very appealing and full of precious pearls.

As for Tim, he was not a usual child. He was not chosen from among the wards of the state. He was entitled to only three chances. But a scar resulting from abuse on his face left him without a family once and for all. "Impossible, invented!" some people said in regard to his story.

In the case of his difficult survival — a homeless man on a bench, who was shut out of society — he found that a judge and a professor who were worthy of their vocation were his "supporters," as he likes to say. But the first person who revealed his beauty to him was a mentally disabled boy who, in touching his chest and his heart said, "You are nice!"

In a similar way, Marie will forever be the barometer and source of the eight loves in your family!

The intensity of the feelings you have shared with us is bearable, thanks to the beauty of your writing. How does it connect so well with our feelings? The happy descriptions give way to Kafkaesque passages, but we escape from suffocation by skipping off into lyrical moments in Mary Poppins' style. We are not experts, but we can confirm that you are gifted — very gifted. And you are right to put this beauty, which Marie arouses and for which she is primarily intended, within the reach of thousands of readers. We will never forget the immense favor of having been the first to receive it.

From both our hearts.

Tim and Martine Guénard

A Before
and an
After

In reading this book, you will, day by day, follow the story of our relationship and family. We have made specific choices that are beyond us now, but, eight years ago, we were certain that we had to make them.

This certitude was so unwavering that it was disturbing, especially since I am not one of those who never doubts.

During the entire time that preceded Marie's arrival, in the style of a diary, I started to write about the days that came one after another and that, little by little, led us to this child who was supposed to be ours. It was the first time that I had written. This desire was a natural progression. On an "ordinary" Monday night, I opened a notebook without knowing where it would lead me. I took up the first pencil that I found. In the middle of the crumbs on the table and the poetry that the older ones were to recite, I wanted to gather these feelings that were invading me — this stream of life that was starting to fill me to overflowing. At that moment, the notebook became a container for me. It was like a big vase that was ready to collect the outpouring that was springing up inside of me.

A thick fog vanished, and an unknown light started to flood our lives. I did not ask why. I did not write about what I was going to do with these notebooks that were starting to pile up and were filled with our story. I did not write "in order to" or "because." I wrote truthfully, without pressure, and without thinking of the reader. I simply used a pencil to describe the dawn that was rising in our new lives, like a painter who dips his paintbrush into a palette to draw the beauty of what he sees.

I wrote out of fear that this flow of life would be forgotten.

These few lines were finally published to form the book entitled *Fallen From the Nest*, whose republication provides the opportunity to say and repeat that there really was a "before" and an "after" for our relationship and our family.

We Became Less Certain

I look at these years that have gone by with a profound gratitude by very often telling myself that we had the best share of happiness. Nevertheless, none of what we experienced had been announced to us beforehand.

We knew that we were going to undergo an earthquake. But all the specialists who were struggling with us to come to our senses were speaking of an earthquake that would be devastating for our marital and family equilibrium. We listened to their theories, which were inflated with scholarship and which they dared to present to us as "the true" reality.

I was disturbed by their certainties. They could show off their diplomas. All that did not ring true for me, for they were talking about a world that was unknown to them. Who can, in fact, talk about the desert, dryness, heat, or the joy of overcoming hardship without having touched dunes covered with ocher sand or having experienced the abysmal silence that makes it possible to hear the beating of one's heart? Can we talk about a disability if we have not stroked a disabled person's cheek, cried with that person as we watched him suffer, or laughed about the unforeseen events that kept happening to him? I now know better why we did not succeed in making ourselves understood and why these specialists did not manage to keep calm. I have often thought that I was not credible because of my youth, energy, and imagination.

But that was not the problem. It was more profound. We had such a hard time communicating. They were anxious about our request. We were anxious about their risk-free life.

We were in two distinct spheres with visions that did not manage to coincide or to converge. They wanted to think. We wanted to live. But living did not mean that we refused to think. It was simply that once we said "yes" to welcoming a different child and allowing it a place in our family, we chose trust. We chose to accept not immediately having all the answers and to allow time to teach us, in a gentle way, what life had to offer us.

That was quite a departure for us! In fact, while remaining stationary, we left for the craziest trip imaginable. We got a one-way ticket. We would have limited the madness of our commitment, but our love for this child exploded every rational explanation.

Today, it is still impossible for me to "explain" this choice of adopting a child, as we were not suffering from sterility. It is impossible for me to explain this strength that was born in us to cherish a "battered" child while we already had six children. It is impossible for me to explain the peace that dwelled in us and that enabled us (my husband Nicolas and myself) to leave on this path that seemed, according to everyone, full of stones and ruts.

It was not out of humanism or masochism that we decided on this child. Before the meeting, we were already experiencing a fatherhood and a motherhood that were growing, taking root, and directing our family's orientation. We knew that love was calling us. We had to cross this "great canyon" where everyone predicted "death" for us — the death of our carefree lifestyle and freedom. If we were crazy enough to take this child in our arms, we would have this "heavy body" depending on us all our lives — a "burden," finally, that would take our availability and independence away.

Everything had to get tough, painful, troublesome, and boring.

We had to endure difficult discussions with specialists and our family! *"We do not choose a disability. We endure it,"* they would tell us. This is the theory that is shared by many people. I simply responded by saying, *"We only choose to love. We do not choose the rest."*

That notorious day, May 24, 2013, was the day when Nicolas and I found ourselves firmly bound to each other in our desire to cherish our little Marie, who was becoming our daughter. We discovered that accepting the disability and feeling her fragility up close was not a dry path.

The days went by. We saw our children's joy in loving this little sister. We "fell" from our certitudes (or at least from those we had been hit with). We discovered in our own flesh that simply loving a person and looking at her as she is was a worthwhile path. I would even dare to say that it is incredibly fruitful. This path leads us to another world. It is an unknown world, or one that is very poorly known, whose richness — in spite of the difficulties encountered — is unbelievable.

This path was so fruitful that our family was enriched by the arrival of two additional children who were wards of the state. They each suffered from a different disability. Marie-Garance, who arrived in 2016, has a severe multiple disability that will make her totally dependent for life. Frédéric, who arrived in 2019, suffers from a pathology in his cerebellum.

We Discovered an Incredibly Valuable World

This value was not limited to our simple family unit once these children were welcomed. It also provoked an explosive richness!

In fact, when our daughter Marie arrived in our arms, we were very happy to know families that had a "different" child. We were able to hold their children close to our hearts, laugh with some parents, listen to their suffering, see them bounce back little by little, and discover the life that awaited them. It is not a life without pleasure, but an unexpected and unforeseen one, with joys that overwhelm you within a different kind of daily life.

These families became our friends.

So, we set forth. With Nicolas, we created an association called "Fallen from the Nest," to bring disabled children and adults to light. We felt moved to hear them and to draw attention to them, and to allow them to talk about their lives and their stories. The world had already spoken too much for them. Nonetheless, they have so much to tell us. We felt that we could, in this manner, help families to experience their disability in a way that was less burdensome and somber.

Two other books were written to collect, once again, this overflow of joys and discoveries that our children brought us. They were also written to reflect on this new world that was offered to us and that spoke a language that was so simple and, nevertheless, rejected.

With some friends, we also created a school to offer these children access to an education that addresses their unique characteristics. It was a small change that had a big impact on the future. The resulting energy made us come alive and led us to build, create, share, and love.

We Wanted to Speak of the Light that These Damaged Bodies Allow Us to Experience

Like a researcher who excitedly proclaims his discovery everywhere, we felt like speaking about the light, joy, and peace that these fragile beings offer us. We could not, in fact, allow people to remain in the profound ignorance that begins to reject fragility. This concept must, on the contrary, become embedded in the heart of our society.

And that is where everything changed dramatically for Nicolas and me. The further we go, in fact, the more we understand that these beings are the true "gems" of our world. It is up to us to discover the magnificent radiance that these battered bodies allow us to experience. It is incredible and amazing.

This discovery, unfortunately, was poorly received. We were treated like liars, lunatics, and guilty people by those who have not made this choice and who asked us to be quiet because it was shameful to them. We spoke freely, but we did not judge anyone.

That Which Shines the Brightest is Not Always the Most Radiant

At the end of 2016, we welcomed Marie-Garance, a petite 16-month-old foster care child and we held her close to our hearts. Marie-Garance suffers from many disabilities. Her medical record is dreadful. Nonetheless, behind the hardness of this endless list of "all that she will never be able to do," every day we discover to what extent she is alive. She wakes us up and makes us understand that we are vulnerable, fragile, and mortal. We often live dangerously when we do not measure our finiteness.

Marie-Garance prolonged the search for depth that she inspired. No two people are alike, just as no two disabilities are alike. Marie-Garance has pointed us to another organization and pushed us toward hospital halls we had never visited before. She made us sit down. She taught us to keep watch by spending many nights near her when she was in respiratory failure. At every moment, everything could dramatically change. We were certain of nothing. We did not know if death would win this game. But we were sure we belonged here — close to her, very close to her — and that we had to live day after day by nourishing ourselves with what was given to us to live. The rest did not depend on us.

Little by little, I understood that the most deserted places are the source of the most infinite riches. In this way, I discovered that what truly shines does not have the most luster.

Marie-Garance's medical record clearly implied that independence was impossible for her and would remain impossible at every stage of her life. By living through these painful moments, we became aware that we were more dependent on her than she was on us. How ironic!

At the end of April 2019, a little boy who was 3 years old enlarged our family again. Frédéric suffers from a pathology of the cerebellum, but his intelligence has not been affected. We discovered a new language mode to try to heal the pain of his abandonment and his physical sufferings that forced him to be fed via a gastrotomy (a surgical opening into the stomach).

Of course, we do not know everything about the disabled person's world. But we have opened some windows that let us perceive a landscape we did not suspect existed before.

"On earth, it is not the opportunities to be amazed that are lacking, but those who are amazed."

This sentence — from Eric-Emmanuel Schmitt (*The Night of Fire*) — appeals to me, and I find it to be so appropriate. I would undoubtedly have been indifferent to it a few years ago, but now, it sums up so well what we have discovered.

Since the notorious day of May 24, 2013, we have been learning every day. The most revolutionary thing has been to discover the strength of amazement. Personally, it is what keeps me alive and gives me a breath of fresh air in each circumstance, even the most painful ones.

Amazement can overtake us in each instant, including on our darkest days. It is the invisible thread that lets us continue to be happy.

I eagerly rediscovered everything — the joy of spending several minutes looking at a bird, the tenderness of seeing our children explode with joy at Marie's slightest progress, and the patience to realize that everything takes more time than you think. I have also learned to accept that everything can overwhelm us and not to exhaust ourselves looking for perfection, but to fill our story with sincere gestures. I have learned that life can be beautiful but hard and that we can squirm to reinvent daily life when faced with unforeseen events that regularly collide with it. We can also allow tears of fatigue to flow when we can't make it and let ourselves fall to the ground and accept finding something else to help us get back up. We can find the childhood joy of running wildly and loving without any limitations and accept that life is crazy. We can let ourselves be overwhelmed by our dreams to avoid being suffocated by narrow reasoning that binds our desires.

It is as if we all had to start over. There were no more performances or overly rapid projections into the "future, tomorrow, or the day after tomorrow." Now, we have become less certain. We have put the excessively rigid education texts into the fire. We have swept away our acquisition of knowledge. We have become free of learning just to agree with knowledge — no more *a priori* assumptions that prevent us from consenting to what life wants to teach us. We have stooped down to the ground, even lower than Marie. She has become our reference, one day at a time, step by step. We have organized the support she needs by looking first at her. We have totally immersed ourselves in her so that we can go forward. She has tamed and adopted us.

Some could be tempted to take shortcuts that are too rapid by telling themselves that our other children were abandoned by having to put themselves on Marie's level. Quite the opposite has happened. Marie has led us to awe and simplicity, and this richness has spilled over onto us. This new way of looking at the world has affected each one of us.

Our Children Have Guided Us Toward a Pursuit of Knowledge

This is the first door that Marie has opened for us. It is to start by looking at the littlest one to let oneself grow, to kneel before weakness, to surrender to what we can't handle, to mourn our weaknesses, and to learn to walk again, and, over and over, to accept returning to the ground to dig deeper.

It is this dynamic, which is almost physical, that has changed in us. We have stopped trying to go further. We have ceased our frenetic race. We found that it was no longer necessary to travel for miles to discover things. Everything was within our heart's reach. It was up to us to make ourselves available to read the messages that were hidden under each little stone that slid under our feet.

This world gives me more answers than I have been able to find in speeches and books.

Discovering this new world has become an inexhaustible source of inspiration in my search for knowledge. It gives me the energy to keep seeking. I, who was foolish in the classroom, have become eager to learn. I was always ready to fool around so I could get out of class. I was much more interested in carving my erasers and drawing my sewing projects than in writing my lessons.

My family journey has allowed me to reconcile myself with what I have learned. It is thanks to my children that I have discovered the desire to immerse myself, with pleasure, into the world of books. I am now eager to learn in order to advance and especially, to try to connect everything that I have learned, heard, and felt.

In fact, everything is connected. Nothing is closed off. This new resonance with life gives me an incredible energy. It all makes sense and leads to creating connections. This new world is so rich!

Every day, I measure the existence of this invisible link that unites all of us by no longer having the feeling of being a free electron alone in a vast galaxy. This link creates a magnificent chain that we call humanity.

Thus, we are all precious, for we are part of a unique and irreplaceable link in this chain.

This Did Not Spare Us from Suffering

At this stage, it seems important to emphasize that this profound joy and peace have not spared us from periods of suffering.

We, like everyone else, have had difficult times — even very difficult ones — of doubt and discouragement during which we have been afraid of not being able to live up to our promises.

Therefore, we do not always have tears of elation flowing down our cheeks. And for good reason; there is no place or situation on this earth where we could seek refuge and be spared from suffering. Infinite happiness cannot be separated from suffering. The consuming quest for life to be happy can, finally, get us lost and have us miss the point. On the other hand, deciding to live by turning to others while accepting our "deserts" lets us discover our true selves and live a deeply happy life.

Of course, we continue to be humans who have limitations. We do not always capture the wonder in life. On some days, we do not have the energy to grow. We sometimes feel like giving up and no longer moving or overcoming suffering and unexpected circumstances.

Life is not magical. It teaches us and does not spare us. These difficult moments of discouragement allow us to remain humble and force us, once again, to take a leap of faith. Feeling weak is always painful, but it is also what makes us strong, as Saint Paul writes (see 2 Cor 12:10).

If life offers us new stages, it also allows us to be free to accept or reject going beyond them. This choice is not always without suffering.

For this reason, I understood that all motherhood goes through a trial by fire. Consenting to this has freed me.

This sentence from Christiane Singer really reverberates inside me: *"Love exists if there has been a tussle, friction, a hand-to-hand combat with Creation, a fight with the angel, and a confrontation with the shadow that lives in us."*

We Are Each Born to Experience a Marvelous Love Story

Our story about suffering and disabilities often provokes strong reactions.

Our gaze is our own. It remains connected to our personal and family history. We are not trying to make impressive speeches. We are simply sharing what we have experienced and the incredible richness that has sprung up in our lives, thanks to these unique children.

Sharing does not allow for comparisons. Sharing brings the story and the experience that each of us, where we are, is living through. Sharing does not aim to give us a unique vision that everyone likes. It simply offers another prism. It opens up another side of our world and gets our minds off ourselves.

Our story does not intentionally lessen the painful stories of other families that are confronted with a disability. Neither does it allow for shortcuts that would dare indicate that we are doing better than others.

There is no "better" or "worse" for us. We are all immersed into this humanity, which we do not know, and whose codes we must decipher. We fight and often lose our footing, but what we are sure of is that our story is the story of everyone who discovers humanity's greatest wealth.

Nicolas and I had to go through a trial of the flesh and of disability to go forward, discover, connect, and, with a new clarity, enlighten everything that we have tasted up until now.

Our vocation has become clear. We have been created to walk together on this path that is our own and that has been designed for us. It has made us grow and has awoken us.

In a word, it is to love till death do us part.

TOWARD A
NEW LIFE

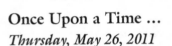

Once Upon a Time ...
Thursday, May 26, 2011

It was 7 o'clock. I was in the doctor's office. It was a mandatory visit to assemble a record of your arrival.

Before leaving to pick up the older children at school, with one arm I grabbed a Maxi-Cosi (a car seat) where Brune, who was 2 months old, was sleeping. Philippine, who was 3 years old, was in my other hand. My car keys were between my teeth. I had only a fingertip left to take a snack, a cuddly toy, some diapers, and a curled-up T'choupi book (a cartoon character) that was lying around, to color with. I blindly grabbed a sample of perfume in a bathroom drawer as well as a spritz on the fly. I put it down. It was a blessing. I smiled with twinkling eyes and slammed the door.

I would later understand that my desire to go toward you was a "call to leave my own land." It was an invitation to open myself up to a new life — the start of an exodus that led me toward an unsuspected future. It was not a coincidence but a genuine opportunity to take hold of another life.

The General Council provided us with a list of several doctors who were referred to us. How were we to choose?

"Am, stam, gram
Pic et pic et collégram
Bour et bour et ratatam
Am, stram, gram ... pic ... dam."
[A children's choosing rhyme that cannot be translated.]

I choose him! He would check our whole family out. There was no possible doubt now that we were headed your way. I was trusting.

I made an appointment as quickly as possible. I explained to the secretary that our children were not yet aware of our progress. We knew that the process would be long. We wanted to protect them. I was counting on the doctor's discretion.

During this meeting, the children were calm and smiling, which I was relishing.

This doctor was gentle with each one. With pleasure, he answered every one of the thousand and one questions that were bursting out. He ended his exam with Brune. She looked at him with big black eyes, as an owl would do. This astonished little face amused me. It could not, in fact, comprehend what this meeting foreshadowed for the family.

When we were leaving, the doctor warmly shook my hand while wishing me a safe trip. This moment was powerful. Time stopped for me. Words could not express our emotion. The children were around us. We were both frustrated with not being able to exchange words. So, we continued to be stuck on this handshake, which was the only means of communication that remained for us to express our feelings. My eyes became more and more misty. He had such a kind look that assured me that our story would come true.

It was certain! I do not know why, but it was certain. This was the unshakable and instinctive certainty of a mother. I promised myself to see him again when we welcomed you.

On the way back home, the pressure dropped — the pressure of preparations that were in full swing, of this random encounter of a "chicken on a wall," and of the sincere and caring glance that the doctor gave me. Tears overwhelmed me like a groundswell. They were sobs of an intense joy that carried me away. As of this day, this precise moment, I became your mommy.

I perceived that it was the start of a beautiful adventure that we could not keep for ourselves. It was an incredible human adventure that pushed us to our limits. It would force us to set aside all our fears and preconceived notions in order, finally, to glean the most important thing, which was to wonder what we were doing with our lives and where this life had to lead us.

An indescribable force attracted us to you like a magnet — to such an extent that we asked ourselves a question: Was it you or us who needed the other?

I have wanted to redo the chronology of this long wait and explain the numerous steps we took and the meetings we attended, and to what extent you were expected. I hoped that when they were bigger, our children would be able to relive this adventure that transported them into another life, turned their daily lives upside down, and changed their existence. May they know why we chose to disrupt their world.

That day, on Thursday, May 26, 2011, I was, first of all, writing this long letter for you — Côme, 10 years old, Baudouin, 9 years old, Tiphaine, 7 years old, Marin, 6 years old, Philippine, 3 years old, and Brune, 2 months old, and of course, for you for whom we were waiting. You would take root in a family whose existence you were still unaware of.

I Chose Love

It seems that you were born in my heart from the outset. From the time I was 6, I longed for adventure. I dreamed of traveling, and of living with someone else, especially if he was different from me. As I was growing up, I was certain that we all had to build our futures for others and with them to the best of our ability.

In 2004, this feeling became more vivid after the birth of Marin, our fourth child. I was ready to welcome another child, a child who was unlike the others, so why not you?

It was an idea that seemed simple at first glance but crazy in retrospect — an idea that I tried to examine rationally. But it became irrational.

And the more time went by, the more I told myself that the idea would go by with it. Sometimes I even hoped to find excuses not to think about it anymore.

Why bother? Would we have the strength to take care of this child for her whole life and ours as well? Could not this adoption become too heavy for our children and our relationship? Did we not risk destroying our family equilibrium?

I could choose to stay on marked paths and find excuses. But I was incapable of building my life on reason while setting my feelings aside. I detected that in choosing to be reasonable, I would let an infinite happiness escape. This was not rational, but I felt it in my gut. I recognized myself in Balzac's words: *"Reason always thinks it is superior to feeling and mocks it [...] Giving reason the upper hand over feeling is the downfall of people with narrow souls."*

It is never "too much" with love! Have we ever seen billboard ads posting the slogan "To love ... with moderation"? It is really the only excess that provides access to the greatest happiness.

I dug deep within myself to find the answer to the essential question that Gustave Thibon asks: *"Love or death — which one is an illusion?"*

Is it love or death that must dominate my life? Is all that I decide to do on this earth done in view of love or of my certain death? Must I preserve myself or keep myself, like a sardine, neatly tucked away in its can, and anxiously wait for my pine box? No! A thousand times NO! I wanted to live for the sake of others without missing out. I wanted to be alive. There was no need to preserve myself. My days were not numbered. Death, for me, is merely a passage to an eternal life. I refused to accept the decree that our society dictates to "take care of yourself." So, not believing in death, I firmly chose love.

You were already there. Love had conquered you. You resonated so much in my heart that this idea continually returned in every moment — exactly like the kicks that your brothers and sisters gave me to remind me of their presence when they were growing in my womb.

... And Your Father Also

The first step was to talk to Nicolas, your father, about this. This procedure was impossible without him.

The idea of becoming your mother had become evident to me. I was afraid of talking about it with your father, fearing that he did not want to go down this road. We knew no one in our family who had taken these steps. We had never asked ourselves about the subject of adoption, since we had no problem having children.

I decided to take some time before sharing this dream with him, thinking that this passion might recede a little. His refusal would be less difficult to bear. But the passion did not go away with time. On the contrary, it took root in my heart. It became urgent for me to talk about it with your father.

Ultimately, we do not calculate the day on which we will reveal our strongest dreams. The heart does not calculate. It beats. I do not know why that, one day, our lips burn so much that they allow the heart to speak. At that moment, we give words to our troubles.

So, on an ordinary day, when we were peacefully together, in the most relaxed moment possible, I spoke to him about you. My heart surrendered.

His answer was quick and obvious; it appeared evident to him also. It was a "YES" that resonated as strongly as the one exchanged five years earlier when we got married. That "yes" proved we were willing to go forward in the same direction, while facing the same horizon.

I remained speechless. I even doubted that he understood what I wanted to tell him. I was prepared for him to say no. Up until then, I had forbidden myself to think about you. Today, I could let my heart dream without fear of wounding it.

Nicolas and I had met on a weekend, thanks to some mutual friends. It was an unlikely first meeting on a railway platform. Nicolas had some Mephistos (a kind of shoe). I had a canary yellow backpack. He was 27. I was 20. The night before this meeting, I was sleeping in the home of Paulette, a very good friend. We did not sleep a wink all night. We were remaking the world, while seated on a carpet from the 1970s. Early the next day, without knowing it yet, I met the one with whom I hoped to build this new world. Ten months later, we were married.

We let this idea grow for six years. We always kept it in mind. The idea of welcoming you had even started to invade my daily life completely. I no longer took a step without telling myself that two little feet would follow me everywhere.

During this time, Philippine was born, and then Brune.

First Steps Toward You
April

After six years of introspection, for the sake of practicality and wanting this dream to come true, we applied to the General Council to obtain the consent for adoption. All these years, when I imagined you and dreamed about you, I wanted, finally, to carry you, feed you, console you, and play with you — to love you.

The first meeting with the Council was in April. Brune was only 2 months old, but we were ready. We knew that the process would be long and would leave time for her to grow up a little before your arrival.

We met with many people who wanted to adopt a child. Each of their stories and motivations were diverse. It was a general information meeting that was meant to explain the different stages to follow.

First and foremost, we put together a file that stated the facts about who we are and how we live. We collected the birth certificates, criminal records, required details about our two families, photographs of the children and ourselves, our proof of income, the explanations about our housing, the proof of a medical check-up with a licensed doctor, our cover letter, etc.

This file was registered with the General Council. We were able to start the journey with a social worker and a psychologist.

Why You?

November

Things were simple for us. We wanted to adopt a ward of the state, a so-called "special needs" child, that is to say, a disabled one — because those children needed a family. There are very few children without special needs. They have no trouble finding parents who want to welcome them. Since we did not have a problem having children, it seemed absurd to seek those who were so eagerly awaited. We did not choose a specific disability. We did not care. We wanted to adapt to your specific needs.

During the many meetings with the psychologist or the social worker, we explained why we waited for six years before setting out on our journey. We wanted to be sure we were mentally and physically available to welcome you, who would be, simultaneously, different and adopted, with all the difficulty that could entail.

When we decided we wanted to adopt you, we had only been married for five years. We did not want to rush. It was a choice that we were making for the rest of our lives. We could take the time to know ourselves better and to continue to move forward together before we set off.

We wondered how you could become our child and find your place among your siblings and how to love you as much as the others but not more than them. You would not have our genes nor look like your brothers or sisters. I was not going to carry you in the literal sense of the word.

So, we asked ourselves what makes us parents today. Do

we love our children because they are normal or because they come from our flesh — from the merging of our gametes?

We are their parents because we are taking care of them and try to love them more each day through the care we provide them.

Love is not magical. It is built every day. We must learn to look at each other to love each other for what we're worth.

We would have to tame you, who would not have our flesh. You would, to us, look like the Little Prince's fragile and mysterious rose. We would have to devote some time to get to know you, discover your needs, shortcomings, emotional language, signs of distress, anxieties, and signs of joy.

As a couple, we decided to set aside numerous activities, commitments, and even our passions for you. That was not difficult. What we renounce carries less weight than you. We knew that we would not be able to reinforce our strength. A hot-air balloon cannot rise if it is too loaded down. We had to rid ourselves of unnecessary things to get to you.

All the practical aspects that were involved in your arrival were by no means a limiting factor. During an interview with the social worker, Nicolas perfectly explained to her that if the child had a physical disability, we would modify the front door to allow for the passage of a wheelchair.

Finally, why you? For us, it was so simple. We were ready to receive you.

It did not matter if you were one of us or if you were perfect. We wanted to love you — with your own special features that made you unique and so rich for us.

You were waiting for a family. We were ready. That was as evident to us as connecting, as in a child's activity book, the duckling to the duck, the colt to the mare, and the chick to the hen. You also had to be connected to a family. As a case study, we could add you to the Noël family and connect these lives to one another for everyone to be happy.

From a very young age, we teach children that every living being is attached to a mother. Wouldn't this logic apply to you? Would you be the exception to the rule? Would nature be so cruel that it would reject all that is different? Would human nature be as cruel as the animal world?

Things are not set in stone. From the first days of your life, your difference was a disability. This would become a blessing since it would let us meet each other.

An Unforgettable Christmas Eve
December

Christmas arrived. We left, as we do every year, to see Nicolas' aunt.

Nicolas' father was a *pied noir* (a French national born in a North African colony). The result of the mixture was jarring. Nicolas unites a great imagination and human warmth to a completely German rigor that is mixed with a limitless energy for work.

The car and the trailer were full. We used the trailer as a pantry during the two days of the trip.

We traveled across France to reach the Pyrenees and the Spanish border. We had a stopover and a short night. We got back on the road before the sun rose to catch the boat in Algésiras. We crossed the Strait of Gibraltar, which seems so ridiculously narrow on a map that we imagined being able to step over it. Realistically, things were completely different. The sea was rough, and we and the boat were subject to some meteorological whims. All eight of us were stretched out on the floor to be in line with the eddies. After a few minutes, everyone was sleeping tight. Nicolas had anticipated this problem by allowing all of us to fast. This was not the case for the other passengers. They were all marching across the deck.

Those 10 days far from home allowed us to regain our strength after these rather turbulent months. Our daily life had been caught up in a dizzying whirlwind of meetings, work, school, meals, telephone calls, and mail, which were indispensable to move the procedure — and the gigantic shopping carts — forward. We felt very distant from the routine daily grind that some people complain about.

After our vacation, the psychologist and social worker had to see the children, who were not yet aware of your arrival. We decided to talk with them about it on the way back.

On December 31, we left at dawn. The car and trailer were still full. But this time, they were filled with tissues, souvenirs, and Moroccan picnic lunches that were prepared with all of the care that Haïda and Khadidja provided. The bread was replaced by some kesra, which is a semolina cake.

The thorough change (as always, there was not enough room for all that was bought) was orchestrated by Nicolas with the precious help of our friends Brahim and Mourad.

As we did on the way to Algeria, we stopped in Spain; but today, the date was special. Everyone chose a package of candy, some chips, and a sparkling drink at a gas station to celebrate the change of year.

Nicolas informed the children that we had some big news to announce to them. We were seated in a circle in the hotel room in the middle of this festive picnic, far from the "five fruits and vegetables" that are strongly recommended by the Minister of Health.

Everyone screamed: "We're going to have a baby! Mommy is pregnant!" Almost, but not quite! "Much better than that," Nicolas said.

We were happy to see them rejoice that the family would be getting bigger. We had hoped to experience this great expectation with them. We wanted you to have real brothers and sisters who were happy that you would be coming and not be hostile to your differences. We did not just want you to come into our family. We were trying to get the children to accept you as one of them and to have your love be embraced through these blood ties.

Nicolas explained our family's grand project to them. I

was very moved to look at this scene. Once again, I measured to what extent Nicolas resonated with this plan. He not only said "yes" to me. He embarked on this crazy wager that still animates him today. Joy crept up on him. The eyes of Côme, Baudouin, and Tiphaine were wide open. They even forgot about their candy. The three youngest ones, on the other hand, did not let go of their "spoils." They were still young, and all that remained abstract to them.

The three oldest children bombarded us with questions through which each one's character appeared. They were very content, but recognized that they were scared. This was quite legitimate. We told them that the path was going to be long. It was not at all certain that we could welcome you, but we were surrounded by specialists who could answer all our questions.

This December 31, which was already odd because of its circumstances, became an unforgettable date for us. Two years later, they would talk to a psychologist about it again. Their hearts were full of emotion.

They were profoundly touched by their father's joy during this announcement. To discover that he only desired to love you, a little "battered" being without a family, made a permanent impression on them.

A YEAR THAT
DID NOT END

A Hopeful Meeting
January

Our request was too "broad" for the social worker who welcomed us. It was a sign to her that our project had not ripened enough. The meeting lasted more than four hours. We were going around in circles. The more we told her that we wanted a child without any conditions, the more it seemed to her that our project was unclear or even crazy. We thought, on the contrary, that our project was solid and thoughtful. It had taken root deep within our hearts for six years.

For us, things were simple, evident, and fluid. That scared the social worker. We, on the contrary, were no longer scared. We had thought for years. We had racked our brains. "So ... a child? Yes. Not one of ours? OK! But how, then? Well ... a child!" It took us six years, finally, to understand that we simply wanted to love "a child" in the most uncomplicated way possible, without any conditions. Is that so crazy?

It is the reverse that seems unbelievable for us. Thanks to these years of reflection, we crossed the barrier of difference, this barrier that stops everything. How freeing this was! But we found other barriers in front of us that prevented us from going forward in this direction. We had the perception of going backwards. It was hard, very hard, and even painful for us to have to understand that our case could only be accepted if we imposed precise conditions on the child whom we wanted to love. We became aware that things risked being more complicated than we thought. We felt as if we were laboratory rats that had to be studied up close.

The social worker referred us to an international adoption medical specialist so that we would have a more precise vision of what a disability is in order for us to be realistic.

This doctor's calendar was full. The earliest we could see him was a year later. What was the use of meeting with him? Our process had to last about nine months. We did not see the point of this consultation that would occur after we got our approval. I decided, nonetheless, to make this appointment and play the game.

I grabbed the telephone on a Tuesday at 11 o'clock and, against all odds, an appointment opened up at 1 o'clock in the afternoon. I was available and without any children at home on that day. I accepted and called Nicolas. He was on the highway. Without thinking twice, he took the first exit to join me. His professional lunch could wait. He, once more, showed how invested he was in this project that we both supported.

We both arrived at the meeting on time. We were, simultaneously, a little stunned and excited by this unexpected lucky break. (I later learned that this doctor consulted only on Tuesdays.) This international adoption specialist welcomed us with amusement for, she said, it was the first time that her calendar allowed her to offer a meeting on the spot.

The meeting with this doctor was very rich. It was an unexpected privilege to be able to talk about you, who were enlivening us so much. She calmly explained that our process and reflections were all acceptable. But we had to adjust our request according to the children we already had. In fact, some disabilities would be difficult for the siblings to experience.

That seemed only fair to us. After having swept away all the possible disabilities, she advised us to restrict our adoption application to that of a child with Down syndrome, who would fit in very well with a large group of siblings. We could adopt a child with an isolated sensory disability.

We would always have a fond memory of this consultation. We felt so little in front of these specialists, who were so close to this project for which we were striving. We listened passionately. We wanted to learn and discover.

This woman was very intelligent and had this great finesse, which is unique to some, of not crushing us and of very kindly listening to us with a profound gaze that was connected to her heart.

Thanks to her listening and her silences, we understood that our process was not nonsensical. It corresponded to one of society's definite demands — children waiting for families. We felt that she believed in us. We needed that. This was one of the incredible meetings that we had along this path toward you. These were invigorating moments that were similar to short truces in a long war.

When we left her, she told us that she hoped to see us again and hear from us. We would not have dared to hope this. We needed these specialists to accompany us, both for the adoption and the disability.

After coming back home, I slipped another business card in your file. That one was, for us, a "Gold Visa Premier Card"!

Thus, little by little, we surrounded ourselves with strong people who made up a powerful team around you.

Was this meeting, which fell into place so rapidly, and this unforeseen encounter coincidental? Or were they providential? We will all call it what we want, according to our beliefs. A verse from Jean de La Fontaine was resonating in me: *"Help yourself, and heaven will help you."* Once more, we sensed that we were not alone.

Yes, we were not alone. This long path to you had been very difficult. I had moments of doubt and even despair. I had often shouted, "Why have you come looking for me in my sleep to disturb my tranquility? And why have you abandoned me?"

But each time, yes, each time, I was lucky to see some

glimmers of light that made me confidently get back on the road.

I had never felt Christ's Love so profoundly. It is an unconditional Love. He chose me? But why? Why did He trust me so much?

From that moment on, my faith took on a personal character. He called me by my name. I agreed to associate with Him.

I decided to go for it. I kept this sentence deep down inside me: *"Have faith."* What good, finally, did it do to be afraid? I was not alone. So yes, I decided to let go completely and to have faith.

That day I decided on my epitaph: *"Life is merely madness in love, so, let us live it well."*

First Chosen Step: Our Original Family

Here is a little family portrait, a typical snapshot of a daily life that was disrupted by all these interviews:

It was 7:13 p.m. Brune was nibbling on scraps of crepes that Côme made. Philippine was speaking all by herself to her imaginary bird, the one who did all the silly things she wanted to do. Baudouin, Tiphaine, and Marin were hitting the cardboard on the rug. What calm! We were enjoying these peaceful minutes and were resting.

This very joyful and lively team seemed ready to welcome you. They were six little educators who would help you develop your energy. We knew, in fact, that your illness made your muscles hypotonic (weakened) from your head to your feet. But the energy of these siblings would increase your skills! This great team joined the people whose business cards we had put in your file. Thanks to their carefreeness and their ability to revel in the present moment without infringing upon their future, they would also help us to go through difficult moments.

And once more, I told myself, "Everything is going

well." It was even going very well! There was no possible doubt about it. We were on the right track.

It would not necessarily be easy every day. Never mind. We were happier than ever before. We were already feeling, in a way that was barely perceptible and indescribable, this happiness that quivered in the depths of our hearts.

The Children's Irresistible Transparency
March

The meetings with the psychologist seemed to go well.

Those with the children did as well, even though they goofed around as much as they could in the worst possible way! They shared their naïve and spontaneous reflections — and we were so afraid of running into an obstacle that we were holding our breath.

The psychologist asked them if they had any questions. Tiphaine answered tit-for-tat that her dad told her not to ask any because he was in a hurry. Ouch!

Nicolas made up for this awkwardness on the fly like a tightrope walker. He explained to the psychologist that the children had asked what a psychologist was. She explained her profession and her role in our adoption application. She tried to make each one talk to get to know them personally.

We were separated from the group, keeping an eye on Brune, who was 13 months old. She wished to inspect every corner of the room. We wanted the children to be as natural as possible and free with their questions and answers. They were not conditioned for this discussion. Marin's new question would display their limitless spontaneity. Sorrowfully and with a furrowed brow, he asked, "Does the child have to be disabled?"

Luckily, the psychologist did not dwell on these sentences. She laughed about them and decreed that each child, who was very much alive, would have a place among the siblings. Phew!

The procedure was underway. The meetings seemed to follow one another endlessly.

Stressed Parents

June 20

The interviews with the social worker took a turn that seemed to be more and more strange. She only stayed for a half hour. She did not ask any questions about how the household functioned. This visit was to be the last one, but she told us that we would have to continue to see each other.

We were shocked because in assessing the past year, which already seemed so difficult, we realized that the first meeting with the social worker lasted four hours. There was a second meeting with the social worker that lasted four hours. This was followed by a meeting in our home, a meeting with the psychologist that lasted four hours, a second meeting with the psychologist that lasted another four hours, a social services visit with the children, a consultation with a doctor who was referred to us, a consultation with the international adoption specialists, hundreds of telephone calls and voicemail messages, and hundreds of files, papers, letters, and emails.

All that to hear now that we were far from being finished? She said we had only briefly touched on the notion of a disability. We had to work on an adoptive parentage. We were breathless and were like two zombies. Suddenly, I was cold. My blood was no longer circulating. It was not even moving, as the famous expression goes. I felt my heart contract. My eyes no longer blinked. They were frozen, wide-open, enormous, and empty. I looked at Nicolas for him to save me from this condition. He immediately understood my cry for help and proposed to the social worker that we discuss the notion of adoptive parentage. The children were calm and playing outside. Nicolas also explained that he took the day off for this meeting. She refused to discuss it with us on this visit on the pretext that she did not want to disturb our family. We told her that we were quickly available for another interview. Her calendar was full. We could not see her before September.

This news did not help my condition. Now I felt as if I was going into a coma. The phrase "nothing before September" provoked a gigantic spasm in my neurons. It was June 29. We were hoping to go before the committee in July. This would allow us to welcome you while we were on vacation. It would be an opportune and peaceful family time to meet you.

We were about to fall backwards.

During her last interview, the psychologist indicated that the project was well defined and that she no longer needed to see us. She invited us to send our "termination letter" to the president of the General Council in view of our going before the committee.

Thus, one of them said that the case was closed. The other one said that our conversations had only started. We did not understand anything.

First Disappointment

June

It was the month of June. We were hoping that our case could be presented to the July committee, but our hopes were dashed. There was an attempt to reassure us by telling us that we must not hurry, that we had time, and that it did not matter how long it took. But we felt like screaming that we had been carrying you for several years and that we were most certainly in a time crunch! This "childbirth" was really taking a long time!

Of course, your waiting time was not accompanied by a hormonal upheaval, just a flurry of questions! This inner maturation led, little by little, to our in-depth transformation, which was discrete but real. We hoped to meet a "Socrates," a master of maieutics (the method of arriving at a new or changed position through a question and answer dialogue), who could help us get outside of ourselves and allow us to understand what was going on in our minds and our souls. Unfortunately, we had before us some "sophists," with their well-established certainties.

The last interview left us feeling moody. What a funny whim it was to want, at all costs, to welcome a different child whom nobody desired!

We sensed that nothing was going forward. We tramped on.

During all these months, we were running, calling people who were likely to advise us (lawyers and associations), writing new letters, and completing files. All that was done without forgetting our six children's daily realities — meeting with teachers for the older children, orthodontics and speech therapy for the others, and vaccines for the youngest ones.

Despite that, nothing discouraged us. I would even say that everything encouraged us, for we really knew that you were waiting for us, sure that you would soon be here and that nothing or nobody could prevent it.

The people whom we had to see to advance our case told us that they were overwhelmed and that their service was lacking personnel. Again we did not really understand. Without being specialists, we knew that it was urgent to provide a family for an abandoned child.

It seemed to us that two opposing logical thoughts were clashing. On the one hand, the people who took care of abandoned children hoped that these children would find a home as quickly as possible. And, on the other hand, the ones who were charged with evaluating the families' aptitudes never had enough guarantees.

Such a Beautiful Meeting
June 29

There was a long telephone conversation with the association that would be given the task, in due course, of entrusting the child to us. It made us realize that our eagerness was not a whim. Our contact person, in fact, explained that many children were waiting for a family and that it was the first time in 40 years that so few families were doing the same thing we were. As I was hanging up the phone, my tears were intensifying, my mother instinct was multiplied tenfold, and I promised myself, or rather, I promised us that I would not give up. I made this promise to my family, to this baby, to my baby, and to our baby whom I would hug one day.

This period was not among the easiest for us. Nicolas suffered professionally from the tense economic climate. But that did not call our project into question. I wanted to recognize his inexhaustible energy and life force, which carried us all, his charisma, his faith in moving mountains, and, particularly, his serenity during an ordeal.

This long waiting period was, in fact, the heaviest trial that we had gone through in 12 years of life together. To see you arrive in our home as quickly as possible had become our primary concern.

The adoption association team hoped that we could meet them as soon as possible As a matter of urgency I organized this consultation on the other side of France. Nicolas took a day off, the children would be taken care of after school, and Brune was going to stay in the daycare center.

We went for a six-hour drive. The tension in the car was palpable. I was excited and impatient. We quickly ate lunch without an appetite in an interstate rest area. We finally approached the place where the association's headquarters was located. The dirt road that led to it seemed endless. There were no longer any sounds in the car. Even our breathing seemed suspended. On each side of this path, a forest stretched

out indefinitely. What a sudden peace and serenity! We parked
the car. There was a parasol pine and 11 little white crosses
planted on the ground in front of us. We later learned that
these were the graves of nine children with Down syndrome
who did not survive an excessively serious heart condition and
of two other children who were very sick when they arrived.
This charitable adoption organization had been criticized
for taking up too much space in the municipal cemetery. It
obtained a dispensation to bury the bodies on its land.

I did not dare look at Nicolas. I saw the tears streaming
down his face. I knew that they were rising in mine. What an
emotion. We immediately questioned ourselves. Why were
they buried in such an undignified manner? Didn't they have
the right to a municipal cemetery? They had the same identity as dogs and cats — a simple hole in a garden, and that
was settled? But what suffering.

Are we really in a developed country? What does
"developed" mean? How can we proclaim ourselves to be
developed if we do not respect all of humanity? Since this
question tormented me, I counted on Wikipedia to find the
definition of this word: "Developed countries with a market
economy (MEDC: more economically developed countries)
are countries where the majority of the population has access
to all basic needs, as well as a certain amount of comfort and
an education." The first definitions only invoked economic
development. The developed countries were those that had
a strong gross national product. We now think in terms of
human development.

This definition struck me. We can imagine how much
their parents must have suffered.

We found ourselves in front of a humble old man. His
gaze was extremely profound. His expression was devoid of
all superficiality. It was without big words and was imbued
with simplicity, gentleness, and seriousness regarding the
urgency of placing wards of the state who had been entrusted
to him.

We conversed for two hours. He cared about his little ones as if he were the father of each one of them. He himself had six children with Down syndrome. So, he knew what he was talking about, but he was silent about it. He did not try to puff himself up or tell us that he was waiting for us or needed us. He explained what we were committing ourselves to in welcoming a child with Down syndrome. He did not delude us. He spoke warmly and truthfully. He explained that Down syndrome has an extremely broad spectrum up to and including a profound intellectual deficiency. It was, for him, like a surprise package. In adopting you, we would not know exactly what skills you would demonstrate as you grew up.

That did not frighten us at all since, for us, life, strictly speaking, is a surprise. Who can affirm mastering his child's future, even if the child is normal? Can we even assert for a given instant that we master our own future?

What was important for our host is that we be present to you all our lives — as a baby, at first, but also as a potential adult. What really counted for him was that we love you as our own child. We were not here to perform a good work or an act of humanitarian heroism.

Someone finally talked to us about Down syndrome in a practical way. How wonderful!

We were tired from all the administrative worries that made us feel as if we were preparing for some kind of graduation. We wanted to talk about practical things. This spoke to me as a mother. These included things like how to give you a baby bottle, how to make you lie down, take care of you, and wake you up. He explained that your extra 21st chromosome made your muscles hypotonic from your head to your feet. Nothing would be natural for you. Patience and love would be needed for you to grow. But he told us that love is inventive. Love knows how to place itself at everyone's service and to meet everyone's needs. In most cases, you would walk, talk a little, and would be able to do manual tasks. You would undoubtedly be very attracted to music, dancing, and theater. He did not tell us more, arguably so that we would not be trapped in a very precise vision of Down syndrome. We were not there to write a thesis on Down syndrome. You would be unique, and we would move gently with you every day. I had been accumulating as much information as possible, for I wanted to offer you what was best. You had already suffered so much despite your young age.

Before leaving, we went to the chapel to engage in private prayer. This chapel was bare and sober — in the image of those who built it. A simple but very powerful sentence, which is engraved above the Blessed Sacrament there, made us burst into tears. It was a truthful sentence that struck us right in our hearts: *"I was waiting for you."*

Second Chosen Step: Philou

Philippine was picking up seashells on the beach. She was arranging them on the sand in "families," as she said! Knives were with the knives, mussels with the mussels, etc. A small periwinkle was by itself. She called it the "adopted Down syndrome child" and chose a family for it. They celebrated, for, according to her logic, everyone was happy.

"But why did you choose this family, Philou?"

"Well, because it is the largest one. They are full of love and want to love the adopted child."

At the age of 4, Philippine understood our process better than anyone.

Our Head in the Mountains and Our Feet in Lake Geneva
July

The busy month of June ended. We left for two months of vacation in Évian. After numerous telephone calls and long negotiations, we accepted two extra appointments during the summer recess. We were assured that, in exchange, we would go before the committee in September.

We were finally seeing the light at the end of the tunnel. We were very happy because the latest news had indicated that we were not supposed to get our hopes up before December. We were counting the days. According to our calculations, we could, with the help of the association, hope to welcome you on All Saints' Day.

If the September committee responded favorably, we would be licensed to adopt a Down syndrome child who was less than 2 years old and a ward of the state, without an ethnic preference. We felt as if the "pregnancy" was coming to an end.

This vacation period allowed us to take care of our family unit, which was really disrupted recently, and to put away the emotions of the past year. We got our strength back.

We made ourselves available for our children as much as possible. We often conversed about the arrival of this future little brother or sister. We listened to their worries and questions. We sensed that they were extremely serene. I took advantage of this by buying an African doll for the girls to prepare them if you came from a different ethnicity. It was so simple for us to love you no matter what your origins were. But we also had to understand that this could be complicated for the children. We did not know. We could not foresee or control everything, so it was wiser to get ahead of the questions and the astonishment. Without instantly calculating it, I realized, as time went by, where the little ones were changing this baby's diaper, playing with her, and cuddling with her — how important it was that they get acquainted with her difference to confront it later. Our greatest wish was that you would become one of theirs. You had to join their group. If that had been the case, you would have had an easier time, for you would have resembled their cherished doll.

Why is there no doll with Down syndrome?

We also took advantage of this vacation to announce this news to our loved ones and to our family. The reactions were diverse and even extreme. Never mind!

Some felt obligated to justify themselves for not having made this choice. Others were indifferent.

On the contrary, our closest relatives joined us to build a fortress of love around the fragile child that you were. They played an important part in our happiness and were there to help us. We were very touched. We needed their support.

Finally, that is how we recognized our true friends! We did not ask them to project themselves into our choices or even understand them, but simply to resonate with us in our joys and sorrows.

In the middle of our vacation, we had someone take care of the children so we could go to Paris for the last two meetings. The one with the psychologist went rather well. The one with the social worker left us with a strange feeling.

Although we were present on the agreed date and on time, after having traveled through France, we were told that she could not receive us because she had an outside appointment. She was not waiting for us to come. The secretary offered us another, much later appointment.

After an hour of waiting, the social worker arrived without excusing herself.

She geared the conversation toward the child's ethnicity. We did not have a preference. We once again explained to her that we wanted to welcome a child, regardless of its sex or skin color.

As we prepared for you, we accepted that you were different and came from other parents. Why would your reception be limited to the color of your skin? Once again, we explained that we were not there to pick a child but to welcome the one who needed us — like a gift, which you accept as it is. It was even truer for you. Your sex, skin color, and disability did not matter. It would be you. For us, loving is receiving another person as that person is and not as we would want that person to be. You would have our name and be one of us as soon as you arrived.

The question of the child's sex kept reoccurring.

These interrogations, which were very brutal for us each time, would end up looking as if a child exists only to satisfy a desire. What color? What sex? A daughter for Mommy? A boy to play soccer with Daddy? And why not also choose the color of its eyes and hair? And not a disabled child, in particular, but a perfect child who corresponded to our dreams? It was strange, even disturbing.

She ended up telling us that it was very kind of us, but she wondered if we put ourselves in the child's place. Of course, we accepted everything. But would the child be glad to have white parents?

Nicolas very calmly answered that we would rely on her expert advice. If she thought it would be traumatic for a black child to have white parents, we would follow her advice. She put that in her file.

I did not dare to tell her that having white parents might be preferable to not having any parents at all.

The interrogation did not stop there. And what if this child had Down syndrome and was blind and black? We were taken aback. What was her point? She asked us if we would adopt the child anyway. Nicolas humorously pointed out that the blindness would be a blessing for this child who would not see that his parents were white.

This interview would continue for four hours.

An Atrocious Start to the School Year
Tuesday, September 4

Summer was coming to an end. The back-to-school season was starting. During this vacation time, we figured that we would have to protect you throughout our lifetime, even when we were retired. Your brothers and sisters would undoubtedly have taken off. Our commitment was certainly a lifetime one, but what a joy it was to give everything to the one from whom everything has been taken.

We were well aware that if we did this as a team, we would not know what the future would hold for us. This two-way street could be interrupted earlier than expected. And even if we stayed together, we would each be alone in facing our suffering and the difficulties that this adoption would create for us. Though we are close-knit partners, we are very different. We do not understand life's obstacles in the same way.

We asked ourselves all of these questions. Now, we were certain that we wanted to live with you every day. We were sure of our choice and calm and clearly understood that our daily lives would never be the same.

The schoolbags were ready, and the overalls were fitted. There were some auburn reflections on these brown heads, which were suffused with the lakeside sun. The little group was ready! After having entrusted the children to their new teachers, we left to see the conclusions that the social worker and psychologist drafted.

In accordance with the adoption procedure, we could consult them, by appointment, before going before the committee. These conclusions would be read at the meeting and would help establish if we were fit to adopt.

After reading for a few minutes, we were petrified. First, we wondered if we were not given the wrong file. We did not understand. We discovered that none of what we said was correctly transcribed. Certain sentences that we are sure we never said were even attributed to us.

For the first time, we felt angry. The previous steps in the process were incomprehensible to us. We did not understand anything. Our feelings were extremely turbulent. We were blamed for something we did not do. My ears were buzzing. There was a metal taste in my mouth. I felt like screaming to claim damages and had the animal instinct of a she-wolf that had been attacked. I wanted to spring up to protect you.

The department head came over to ask us if everything

was all right. Feeling weakened, I looked at her. My eyes could not hide my great suffering. I asked her if she was aware of the conclusions that concerned us. She said that she was and was a bit embarrassed about it. So, I sent her question back to her. How can we be doing all right? I was trembling. With my voice wavering, I explained to her that we had opened ourselves up for hours. We had opened our hearts and told our story only to have it be trampled on.

Nicolas did not want to go into the details. In moments of great suffering, he becomes like a robot. His sentences are as streamlined as possible. There are no verbs or complements. There are only interjections that ask for the way out — as if he needs air to breathe again. He asked the department head how to deal with these reports that we were disputing. She told us that we were entitled to respond to them. What a relief!

It was Wednesday. We had until 6 o'clock in the evening on Friday to bring all the written comments that we thought would be useful. The committee would study them on Monday morning before giving us feedback.

It was also possible for us to express ourselves before this committee for 10 minutes. Wanting all the odds to be in our favor, we told them that we would be there.

When we left the General Council, we were still reeling from the shock, but not completely discouraged. Nicolas regained the upper hand right away. There was no time to hesitate. We were lucky to be able to explain ourselves. The two remaining days were precious. We had to make sure that the committee could deliberate on the elements that we thought were real.

Nicolas canceled all his meetings to dedicate his time to our right to reply. We went through the conclusions of the psychologist and the social worker step by step. It was an enormous job, but we were not discouraged. Once again, we did not know where we drew this strength from or, rather, if we knew that we were not alone. This strength attracted us to you like a magnet. This new trial brought us together more powerfully.

That evening, when the children were in bed and after we had worked on our case, silence prevailed, just as after the announcement of a death. We were not really aware of it. We did not feel like laughing, speaking, listening to music, or having the television on. We were both in our heads, turning the story upside down, and trying to find the "why" that led to these conclusions.

After several hours, we found ourselves facing the mirror in our bathroom while mechanically brushing our teeth. Nicolas stopped dead in his tracks. Looking petrified, he said: "I feel as if I've experienced a miscarriage of justice. I sympathize with all these people who are in prison for a mistake they didn't make. What if tomorrow, our children were taken away in exchange for perjury? What have we got left to save them?" That day, we felt like liberating ourselves from these boundaries where we could not express our ideas and choices. We were thirsting for the freedom to think.

In seeing Nicolas suffer in this way, I understood that he was already your father.

That was a big comeback. Our friends did not see us, whereas it was normally an opportunity for reunions after being separated for two months. We did not even have time to make two or three phone calls to explain what was happening to us. We got right to the task at hand. As soon as the indispensable daily tasks were done, we unceasingly prepared our explanations about who we were and what we were hoping for when we went before the committee on Monday. Our nights were short — very short. We worked until 4 o'clock in the morning. After a brief break, we got up to prepare the little group. Please be in a good mood!

After coming back from school one morning, I found a little note that was written in haste on a sheet of a torn notebook. It was deposited on the doorstep, along with some hot croissants: "We are worried. We are not seeing you. Is everything okay? We are here if you need us." This was the gift of two adorable little fairies, which was full of tender kindness. It soothed our hearts when we were feeling down. The croissants were so comforting when we were neglecting ourselves a little. What fuel to clear your mind!

We urgently called the specialists who were close to our family. These included our pediatrician and the speech therapist — those who looked professionally at our ability to take care of our children. All, without exception, assured us of their support and, in a few hours, filed a report testifying to their vision for our family. We did not know at all if this would be an asset for our case, but we had to try everything. At this point, we didn't risk much. Nicolas, who is very pragmatic, estimated that we had about five chances out of a hundred to make it, but that we had to pursue every opportunity. This was his ultra-positive side.

We did not have time to proofread. It didn't matter. We wrote from our guts. There was no need for big phrases or specific qualifications. We were speaking of love. We would take care of this child. We didn't study a lot or look for major adoption theories on the internet. We drew our arguments to defend you from the depths of our hearts. At any rate, it was useless to look very far. Before embarking on the elaboration of our right to reply, I made an absurd argument. If what we said was transformed or omitted, it would be enough for our defense to write it in black and white ourselves.

On Friday, at 6 o'clock sharp, our documents were submitted to the General Council. After 48 hours of work without respite, we delivered these items on time: our observations on the reports of the psychologist and the social worker as well as an open letter to the members of the approval board. We appended the testimonies of our family's specialists.

Here is the letter:

September 7
Ladies and Gentlemen, members of the committee,

We did not originally plan to address you in this way, but the reading of the two reports on Tuesday literally petrified us and made us, for the first time, envision the possibility of a denial of approval. We do not claim, via these different writings, to free ourselves from this risk, but only to be sure that your opinion will be formed by having a more precise knowledge of our project.

We'd like, first of all, to thank the different members of Yvelines Foster Care for their availability. We also want to thank them because they let us make our project grow, especially with regard to the definition of disabilities that we are able to accommodate, in light of our family's size.

Our undeniable eagerness, which is evident in both reports, is the tangible sign that our project is ripe and that we are looking forward to welcoming this child.

We are fully aware that the adoption of a Down syndrome child or one who has a unique sensory disability, will force us, even more than for a biological child, to be very attentive and sensitive to the least warning signs of suffering that are connected to its abandonment and disability. We will try to adapt to this child's ways of communicating and to decipher its uneasiness (refusal to eat, insomnia, withdrawal, etc.). Our pediatrician, as well as all professionals who are following our family, will help us in this extreme vigilance as to this child's follow-up.

Likewise, we will be extremely attentive to the relationships of our other children, who must not, in any case, be affected by a parental choice.

It is truly evident that, considering the love and care that it is advisable to bring this child, we cannot anticipate another pregnancy today. We don't wish to insert this child among his siblings. We want to put it at the forefront, to take time to rebuild the family unit around this child, who is so little and weak, and has already experienced too much suffering for its young age. It is inconceivable to imagine this child already as a big brother or big sister. Let's allow this child the time to learn to live together. We are not in some [state of] "child bulimia." All our children, in their own right, must find their own place among their siblings. Currently, this is our only preoccupation.

We are well aware that this disabled child, especially if it has Down syndrome, will live with us for the rest of our lives. Even if it is, so far, difficult to look ahead as long as we do not have a more precise idea of its degree of autonomy, we fully understand that we will not have a retirement life similar to others.

There will always be risks that we have perhaps not understood enough. But, in the same vein, haven't we taken a risk by choosing to have four children in four years and six children today? Those in our family who did not understand these births that are close together are those who, today, are scared by our project.

Our only motivation, the one which made us risk getting married 13 years ago, the one which made us have six children, and, especially, the one which has led us to carry out this particular adoption project, is love. And our love has, each time, been more developed and enriched when each new child arrived in the family.

Today, our family, our loved ones, our village, the daycare center where a place is reserved for us one day a week — everyone waits for this child's arrival. This is without mentioning its brothers and sisters who speak about it every day among and around themselves. We have even bought an African doll for our two youngest daughters to prepare them for the possible arrival of a child whose ethnic origin is different.

Today, we are mentally and materially all set to welcome this child, while being well aware that there is a bit of a leap into the unknown.

In conclusion, we give you these words of Gustave Thibon (an excerpt from *Jacob's Ladder*, Brussels, 1942):

"The person who takes less of a risk is, here on earth, the one who is the closest to nothingness."

Risk is made to be taken. We all carry in ourselves what is needed to overcome the risks which our natures or vocations expose us to.

The greatest risk is a function of the highest destiny. While he was dying, Socrates was happy with the risk of immortality. Blaise Pascal pushed man to the highest bet.

We all exercise caution according to the nature of our heart's treasure.

Real prudence has two eyes. One is fixed on the goal to be attained. The other one is on the risk to be taken. It sees it through to the end. This is why it knows how to confront the risk.

False prudence is, in a way, somewhat dazed. It has only one eye pointed on the risk. It does not see beyond the risk. This is why it refuses to take it. Being deprived, at the same time, of the healthy gaze that sees the goal and the healthy tendency that leads to it, it only has one desire — escaping risk at all costs. People are then destined to stagnation or regression. They dream only of a shell or a guardrail. Their lives are transformed into an immense undertaking of assurances against every risk.

There is no worse imprudence than this false prudence. By wanting to preserve ourselves too much, we destroy ourselves. People who, to preserve themselves better, retreat into lower parts of themselves, are crafting their own destruction, for they are acting against a central requirement of nature and life. They are irreversibly compromising the lesser good that they are claiming to save. In all domains, people must choose, not between security and risk, but between an open risk, which is full of promises, and a risk that is without compensation and without an exit. For, there is no stable landing here for them. The refusal to climb increases the chances of falling. False prudence substitutes the sterile risk of egotism and death for the fertile risk of life and love.

Thanks for your attention.

Take note: Please excuse the nonacademic style and different typos that could be in all these documents. They were written in 48 hours right in the middle of going back to school with six children.

First Hearing Before the Committee
September 10

All that remained was the weekend to prepare ourselves for the hearing. We each examined our personal motivations and the sincerity of our commitment to you.

Nicolas developed his conception of the father's role and his thoughts on the future of the child when we will no longer be there. He showed his willingness to prepare its legal and financial future as well as possible so as not to impose a burden on its brothers or sisters. He did this so that its siblings would be free to take care of the child or not. In any case, we did not want them to experience the consequences of our choices. Nicolas was really anticipating the child's future, and he talked to me about the fruit of his thoughts.

He also explained our readiness, for it seemed that the psychologist had poorly transcribed our message: "Our eagerness to see the adoption quickly become real is, evidently, hardly connected to the possibility of future pregnancies. We will allow time to love this child. We are merely more and more impatient to get our approval, considering that our project has come to fruition. Isn't it legitimate to be in a hurry to welcome this child, since it is so eagerly awaited?"

Nicolas concluded his intervention with these words: "Since Tuesday afternoon, the day when we found out about these two reports, being well aware of the consequences that they could have for our future child's arrival, we, as a couple have been going through the biggest ordeal that we've experienced. Just this morning, we realized to what extent we were united. It took all these days and nights up until 4 o'clock in the morning to prepare these conclusions. Today, we want to tell you again that we are ready for this child's arrival. My wife and I and its brothers and sisters are waiting for this child. By our periodically talking about it, a village is also waiting for it."

I asserted that my emotional availability for this child that was going to be ours was complete even if I did not carry it in my womb for nine months. I practiced my role as a mother every day in the care I gave my children. This child will surely be different because of its origins, the suffering it experienced when it was abandoned, the months it spent in a children's home, and its disability. But we will be there, surrounded by specialists to try to fill in the gaps. Yes, the child will be different. It will need its own care. But its brothers and sisters, although they come from the same siblings, are all very different. This is the magic of the genome!

I also firmly insisted on the fact that I did not at all doubt my ability to love you. You would certainly be my child.

On Monday at 9 o'clock in the morning, Nicolas and I sat behind a very simple table. We were glued to one another. Nicolas was on my left. We were in front of six people who were about to judge our motivations and the credibility of our project.

I made a point of speaking unambiguously, for the conclusions about me that I read lacked clarity and truth. The social worker wrote that I "felt pregnant." I humorously asserted before the committee that I wasn't lactating! I was not confusing carrying a child with carrying a project.

Yes, welcoming you was close to my heart. We fought for that. But we did not leave our mental health there. We knew how to maintain a balance.

It was not easy to reveal our point of view. The arguments of the social worker and the psychologist, to which we tried to respond, were heavily exaggerated: "They are too young, a little too dynamic, and too passionate." Much anxiety about our project was often noted, for "Mrs. Noël hopes to give the child back to its biological mother." How could I have said such a thing? I knew that your biological mother did not feel capable of bringing you up and that she was honest and clear enough in carrying out this act of abandonment. And so, would I, who had hoped for several years to carry you in my arms, have done all that just to return you?

We explained what we thought we had clearly indicated to the social worker. If you wanted to find your origins, we would do everything possible to help you in this process, since our only wish was the happiness and blossoming of our children in truth and freedom. How would such a process challenge our adoptive parenthood? Did we have to consider you to be the object of our whims or as a person in your own right — a person whose growth I would be responsible for so that you would completely and freely fulfill yourself, in light of your uniqueness?

We were not at all ambivalent about our ranking as parents. You would be ours and would appear in our family record book. We would not be opposed to your searching for your biological parents if you felt like doing so. We did not wish to hide your story. We also responded, when we were asked the question, that if you wished to change your name and take back your biological parents' name, we would not oppose this. Our children, whether they are biological or adopted, are full-fledged human beings. They are not our property. We have the task and the joy of having them grow up in love and truth.

Our time to talk was up. In the end, 10 minutes was a lot. The jury thanked us. We left the hall. We were relieved to have been able to express ourselves freely. We did not at all know if our speech touched them, but we were satisfied to have been listened to.

This marathon was done. We had to wait patiently for the deliberation's results. Daily life returned to normal.

A Registered Letter with a Disappointing Announcement
September 22

The following weeks were long, although we were very busy. The wait was endless. I watched for the mail carrier every day.

The mail finally arrived.

Considering that the social worker had issued an "unfavorable opinion" and that the psychologist had issued a "reserved opinion," the licensing board wished to postpone the case in order to conduct complementary psychological investigations. This was, precisely, "to deepen the reflection on the distinctiveness of adoptive parentage."

Nicolas was reassured. In view of the disastrous conclusions of the social worker and the psychologist, he did not think we could have received a better response. The story was not finished. There was a silver lining. Nicolas came back to life. He left, just as he did on the first day. We were, once again, back on track.

My feelings were different. I really wanted a positive response. The route taken certainly suggested a refusal, but I truly, in my heart, was hoping for a reversal of the situation.

Our hearing, in my opinion, had gone well. For me, the time was long. Your absence weighed on me a little more each day. I was overloaded with all these meetings. I read this phrase once, twice, and three times — "to deepen the reflection on the distinctiveness of adoptive parentage."

The letters and words spun around in my head. They seemed stupid and senseless. I even started to laugh about them. I pronounced this phrase rapidly, in a solemn tone and with a shrill voice — a voice with a Southern accent and with an accent that was "so British." I made this phrase come alive, for it meant so little to me! I put it in context. Outside of this context, it seemed incredible. When people would ask me why we adopted you, I would proudly respond: "We have deepened our reflection on the distinctiveness of adoptive parentage!"

Why do we want to intellectualize maternal love? My brain was no longer functioning. My heart took over. I was really sad and tired. You had already lived in my heart for so many years. There was not a day that I did not think of you.

It Was Not a Definite Refusal — The Fight Continued

October 4

We were once again on the train platform, with tickets in hand. The children were being taken care of. Nicolas took yet another day off. This time, the train brought us to Paris to meet a psychiatrist who was chosen from outside of our department in order to form an objective opinion — provided that objectivity was called for in this kind of process.

We were not as enthusiastic as last year when we came to our first meetings. Then, we were excited, so happy to present our dream, and eager to learn and move forward with this adoption. Today, we were a little weary of having to repeat the same things.

Through an unfortunate twist of fate, in the corridors

of the Parisian subway, some immense posters that favored the adoption of dogs and cats exhibited their slogan: "A family for Christmas." This was really hard to see. For me, this media coverage rapidly resulted in disgust. Did dogs and cats have more of a place in our society than sick children who were without a family?

I stayed there among all these people who were circulating in every direction. I was completely frozen and dazed in front of this poster. My tears were flowing uncontrollably. I was being shoved and bumped. I did not feel anything and was completely paralyzed. I felt like shouting, "Why, but why?"

This freeze-frame only lasted a few seconds. I was coming to my senses. I dried my tears on the back of my sleeve. Calmly, but more determined than ever, I rushed into the Parisian subway surrounded by this anonymous crowd.

The first meeting with the psychiatrist focused on our emotional past — our parents, brothers and sisters, our studies, and how we met. (I sighed thinking about it.) This happened one more time. But we would play the game again. You really deserved that!

The psychiatrist was aggressive toward me. She did not understand why we had six children. She wondered how we managed this big family. It was tiring, if not exhausting, to have to justify ourselves at all times in order to inspire trust. We did not think that in going through this adoption process, we would have to justify our choices as a couple over and over. Why were there so many children, and why were they so close together?

The interview lasted an hour, after which we gathered on a Parisian sidewalk. We were full of energy. We had the impression of having failed at everything. Our last chance seemed to have flown away. How frustrating it was, after all that we had been through.

"Why did you say that?"

"Why do you never let me talk?"

We were screaming at each other and were exhausted. We were feeling so close to the goal. We were so close to each other and really felt like partners during this whole process. Nonetheless, we never argued as much as at this time!

In reality, we had to come to this point. There was no longer any space between us. To get to you, we had to be anchored to each other. We, in turn, intimately surrendered ourselves, in front of each other, to psychologists and psychiatrists for months. There was no secret between us. After each meeting, we mutually corrected ourselves so we could do better the next time. Without objecting (at least, almost, as far as I'm concerned), we accepted each other's critiques.

This was a difficult exercise in humility, but we had to be able to question ourselves over and over. Otherwise, what was the point of going to you? We could not arrive with a heavy heart that was filled with pride, but with a light one, which was not vain.

So, the times that we bonded with each other were necessarily interspersed with stormy moments. We learned how to get to know ourselves in depth by facing adversity. We measured our limits, weaknesses, and shortcomings. This was another example of a painful exercise in humility. We emerged stronger, for we tried to address our failures to avoid relapsing.

We worked like crazy, ate in a hurry, and slept poorly. We were wound up. But we were sure of our love for each other and of our shared commitment to you.

Our arguments were temporary. We needed each other too much. With all that we had just endured, we were even more united for life. We had to get through these difficulties. We were well grounded in reality, not seated on a soft cushion where every bird sings the Angelus.

Nicolas and I had resisted these shocks, but this was only a beginning. We would still need a little patience and a lot of strength. We decided that we would remain united for life for you. Offering you a home that could explode was out of the question. We had to be even more sure of each other. You had asked for nothing, let alone that we add extra suffering to yours.

It was not through pride, determinism, or relentlessness that we decided to pursue our process, despite the difficulties. It was simply because you were already in our hearts. We already loved you. We were your parents. Finally, we were fighting for you, which was legitimate.

Some people suggested that we stop because this was so complicated. For them, it was a tangible sign that this path was not made for us. We had to give up on you, without whining. We had to accept kowtowing to these conclusions that did not reflect our history.

I started to think about our real intentions. Were we taking pride in the fact that we failed to graduate or because we already loved you?

People can cause trouble when they are unable to understand other people's dreams. They dump their fears on you.

But it was certain that you were already our daughter. Other people's inquisitive eyes did not matter. This was only the beginning. Your difference surely provoked some glances, certain behaviors, and strong words.

I understood that this long path toward you was not useless. It allowed me to go through an essential new stage of letting go of worrying about what others say, which is so powerful and destructive.

I was climbing a new step to freedom.

Our first meeting with the doctor was difficult and destabilizing. A few minutes after this "lightning" on the sidewalk, we went into a Parisian bar. I will always remember this scene. My tears were flowing all by themselves in front of my sandwich, which I was not able to touch. I was distraught and aware that we were deadlocked. Each time, we both found ourselves without any other resources — besides our handbags and coats — to talk about our lives in front of specialists who were supposed to evaluate us. But they missed the main point, which was the group that animated our days, our vacations, and our life!

How were we to discuss our lives, occupations, and structures by ignoring our children, who determined them? How were we to be convincing? We responded peacefully to the questions while sitting in an armchair. The woman in front of us was looking at us with eyes that resembled flying saucers. She seemed so astonished that I imagined there were thousands of bubbles above her head containing question marks. She must have noticed the hubbub that was caused by six infants, the endlessly spinning washing machines, the numerous ironing boards and laundry to sort and fold, the kilos of dough that were baking, the doors that were slamming, the older children who were doing their work alongside the ones who were messing around, and the youngest one who was always throwing her plate of mashed potatoes on the floor from her high chair. For her, it appeared as a life of daily constraints that were unceasingly renewed. I sensed that she couldn't take this anymore, that her brain was overloaded, and that she was even exhausted for us. She often breathed by repeating, "But why? Why so many children who are so close together?"

She noted the birth dates — 2000, 2002, 2003, and 2004. She was marking time, looked at us, and collapsed. She went back to the last dates, which were 2008 and 2011. She paused again and observed me from every angle. Drops of sweat were dripping on her forehead. She looked at us. We were very cool, calm, and collected.

We had traded our old sweaters that were decorated with the runniest kisses for casual wear for this meeting. She told us that we did not seem to have six children. She did not manage to link her own conception of a large family to the image that we gave her and to our talk. But we do not conceptualize life. We live it!

We did not look like her idea of a couple with six children. Things are very coded in France. Fantasy cruelly lacks imagination. People are put in boxes. They are given indelible labels that shrink life — undoubtedly, to calm people's fears. People are not welcomed as they are. They are stuck in the conceptualization that others have of them. This considerably diminishes conversations.

During this interview, I felt trapped in preconceived ideas that had nothing to do with our real life. I felt as if I were mimicking a life that was ours. It was very oppressive. I felt like a cow, as if I had been branded with a red-hot number that provided information about me.

Of course, that must have been dizzying for her. In two minutes, she slapped 13 years of our lives onto a piece of paper, whereas our family took shape little by little and day by day. Six children were not suddenly thrown at us.

Finally, why were they trying to understand us and project themselves into our lives? Wasn't their work simply to know if we were capable of welcoming another child? I was, again, disappointed to find myself in front of a "sophist." Seemingly, she could write her conclusions before meeting us. It was enough for her to know our "pedigree." She pulled open the corresponding drawer, and the conclusions were already there. It was very frustrating.

I was still annoyed in front of my sandwich. I told Nicolas that we would never make it as long as they did not see our lives as they really were! They absolutely had to have images that corresponded to our reality. It seemed as though they based their opinions of our life on their vision of our reality. If we tried to ignore this, we could say all that we wanted. We would be wasting our time. We could go from specialist to specialist. It would be endless. We would always come back to the same point.

Once again, Nicolas refused to admit defeat. After a moment, we were quickly back on top. Nothing was decided yet. Our vision of this meeting was subjective. The psychiatrist did not tell us anything that could make us think everything was lost. Did she perhaps seem aggressive because she was trying to push us into a corner? We knew how to remain calm. There was no evidence to suggest that we were unsettled. There were no tears being shed or strong words.

We decided that it was too early to draw any conclusions. There was still an opportunity. It was up to us to grab it! Now that we knew our contact person, we could prepare ourselves for the second round.

On the Sofa Again
October 22

The last session with this psychiatrist took place a few weeks later. Meanwhile, we rested and recharged our batteries. We knew that it was the last one and that, after this doctor's conclusions, the committee would have to make a decision. The procedure, while complex, did not, at this stage, offer any other way out.

This time, the climate was more serene. We had to address the reasons why we wanted to adopt. She rapidly overlooked the fact that our process could be driven by a desire for humanism and a strong sense of altruism. Our heart can, in fact, be stirred by altruism, an ideology, or humanism. But a stirring of the heart is temporary. More is needed for a project involving our whole life. We do not love through the use of reason, pity, a desire to save the world, or to respond to a hurt. We love people for who they are. Our goal was not simply to provide care for this little being. We wanted to love you as our child.

She seemed empathetic during this second meeting. She said she was amused and aware of our dynamism and the good relationship that Nicolas and I had. She seemed convinced of our great love for children. Those were her words. I even told her during our discussions, "Doctor, we all have a sudden whim. For us, it is children. So take that into account, and accept our request."

She flashed a smile and said that she agreed with

everything we stated. Everything seemed to be easy and without a hitch. Nonetheless, she indicated that this would not be possible. But why?

"You are very nice, but you have enough work with six children. Moreover, your children are too young."

But what did she care about our workload at home? We weren't there to talk about that. There were only five minutes left to sharpen our arguments in order to turn the tide.

Yes, our children were young. This was a reality that we couldn't deny. But adoption was like an addition for us. This addition would have a better chance of fitting into our family before it was overwhelmed by the onset of adolescence. Our children were close to each other. Brune was still young, but that was a blessing because you would be adopted. You could be part of the next logical step for these siblings in the making. You could blend in with them much more naturally. She told us that we were atypical and that our project was also. That goes together, doesn't it?

She smiled again and repeated that what we were saying was right. She promised to file a report within no more than 15 days, but warned us that her conclusions were nuanced. There was much at stake for her. She did not want to make any mistakes. She assured us that she didn't mean to harm us.

We believed it. This was probably because of our craziness, youth, and gullibility! But a month and a half went by, and there was still no action. There was no news. We were unable to make plans for Christmas.

This was a very hard period. It was difficult to see that some of our loved ones didn't see the magnitude of our suffering in the face of this case that was not advancing. They said: "But this is not serious. You are still young. You have time," and "Perhaps it's better this way," and "You can have other children naturally. You'll have your seventh little one."

I was still dazed. I wanted to reply that, for you, the time in our children's home must be long and that my goal was not to have seven children. My body matched my head and heart. I couldn't bear another child. You were the only one we were waiting for.

It was also difficult to respond when asked to measure your chances of having six children.

The problem was not to obtain something. We were speaking of a child without a family.

It was also difficult to hear our loved ones advising us to surrender and accept this waiting time. We agreed to let go. It was the centerpiece of our commitment. We decided to say "yes" in seeking you by agreeing not to master everything. Practically speaking, all our projects had been suspended for two years.

We had been picking up the telephone for two years so we could get mandatory summons to interviews "at the right time," that is to say, at 6 p.m. That is when the bath water was draining out and a voice at the end of the hallway was shouting, "Mommy, are you here? Can you dry me off?" although I had been available for the whole afternoon! We organized our vacations at the last minute when they were not finally canceled for impromptu meetings.

To surrender does not mean accepting anything.

We could not accept that our words were twisted, and that reports were drafted more than a month and a half after our visit. How could our contacts transcribe our statements accurately, considering the large number of people they saw every day?

Luckily, time and again, our close friends supported us. They even suffered with us. It was hardly believable! We once again realized that our true friends were always present in both adversity and joy. It was a blessing that there were so many of them. We truly needed them. We really require kindness in moments like that. We create true relationships in revealing our sorrows.

All these people multiplied little signs of affection, according to their temperaments. These included a little text message, a long telephone call, an email, an unannounced visit, misty eyes when school got out, a hand on your arm, an "I love you, and I believe in you" that slipped into our ears. Oh yes, we needed this.

Some offered to write testimonial letters. So, we solved the world's problems at the back of a parking lot after having dropped the children off at school. People started talking, confiding in each other, and sharing their point of view. They learned of us via a third party and came alongside me to tell me that they were with us! These were new, spur-of-the-moment companions who dared to have atypical ideas in a world where everyone had to be identical. We lost friendships and made new ones. Spontaneous conversations provided a lot of richness. We had some beautiful encounters that would not have happened in other circumstances.

That is what remained in my head and heart, now that everything was done. The rest was history and had slid away.

The Flakes Fell
November

It's almost Christmas! Whatever our beliefs, we all, or almost all, gather together for the great celebration while also keeping in mind the most deprived. One question tormented us: Would you be with us in front of the fir tree, this fir tree that sparkled with the love of your brothers and sisters, parents, and family? You belonged here with those who loved you so much, just for who you were.

There was still no news. We decided to call the General Council. It was a delicate task. We were afraid of slowing the process down. But, on the contrary, we ignited things. It all kicked in. We waited for a registered letter. A phone call announced an urgent referral to the committee.

Nicolas ran to refer to the psychiatrist's conclusions before seeing this new committee. They were, once again, disastrous. Nothing that she promised to note had been done. We also wondered about the date that appeared on her letter. It was such a shock that Nicolas literally lost his voice.

The first part of the conclusions, which was very factual, was positive:

"They are a harmonious couple who share the same ideas about the family and the same human values [...]. It seems that, currently, the psychoaffective and cognitive evolution of each of their children is harmonious."

What came next dismayed us:

"What strikes us during these discussions is the existence and unchanging nature of their project, which is never questioned during the evolution of their life as a couple. It is purposefully presented as a goal to be attained in the name of self-sacrifice and welcoming the one who is the weakest [...] This is a very intellectualized process, which is based on the achievement of an ideal that leaves little room for the real child [...] How will they build the filial relationships with a child whose adoption was based more on a humanitarian process than a child's real desire? [...] Their understanding of Down syndrome remains cut off from the context of daily life."

How were we to stay calm by reading this report? This moral violence had a physical impact. Nicolas could no longer talk about the day. He became completely silent, which was an involuntary defense against the anger that was gnawing at us. Our limit of tolerance seemed to have been crossed. For the first time, I was afraid of losing my husband in this fight.

I forgot my moods while facing Nicolas' very strong reaction. I forced myself to be strong. We could not fall apart. He was suffering enough. I could not add my worries to his today. In this way, we functioned like a pendulum that permanently tried to keep balanced. When one caved in, the other one would not allow it to fall. We had to be there for each other. Either we cried, or we were the other person's crutch. We moved forward together, as a team.

I got busy putting the house in order and preparing meals that he preferred so that he would come home to a welcoming, non-hostile universe at night. Everything had to be ready. The children needed to be in bed. I understood that he would need peace and that his silence, in particular, had to be accepted. He needed to be alone. These little extras silently showed him that I was there for him.

The next day, Nicolas was standing strong. He got his serious, manly voice back. He was ready to make it heard as strongly as it needed to be for you!

We sat down to set the schedule for the upcoming days. It was Wednesday. Nicolas had to fly to Morocco for a few days to be with his aunt, who was suffering from a pervasive cancer. This trip was anticipated. We got the tickets and chose not to cancel them.

I took care of our response to the psychiatrist's conclusions, with the help of a little fairy, once again. The final deadline was in two days!

Second Committee Meeting
December 10

On the following Monday, Nicolas landed, as anticipated, at 10:30 a.m. At 3 o'clock in the afternoon, we were once again before the committee. The people who formed it were different from last time, but they received us warmly so that we would feel at ease to state our wishes. Philippine, who was 4 years old, accompanied us. She was our case's living witness. She was there to represent our "real life," the connection between real life and words, the window that was partially opened on our reality. During the 10 minutes that were given us, she was drawing without making any noise. She sometimes glanced at us and smiled.

Each one of us prepared what we wished to say. Our goal was not to repeat everything point by point. We had already done that, and the committee had our entire file in their hands.

Nicolas decided to highlight the tangible elements that

we could rely on about our material and psychoaffective situation. The list was long and concluded in this way:

"In a nutshell, according to the three specialists whom we have met, the financial and material aspects are not a problem. The available time for this disabled child is clearly displayed. Although we have six children, my wife and I are considered to be balanced, united, and harmonious. We've had a much harder time being understood about subjective criteria, a humanitarian approach, an adoptive parentage, our children being too young, a disability that is not sufficiently understood, a psychoaffective approach, the child's subjectivity, and our readiness. We have come back to these different points through the different notes that we have produced when reading each report. We have thought much about trying to find explanations for the distortions between our thoughts and claims and what is written in these reports. From a practical point of view, we really regret not having been recorded so that we could resolve every ambiguity. Beyond these practical difficulties, we think that the three persons whom we have met are not able to conceive of the adoption of a disabled child, as we have six biological children. Is there a typical family to welcome these disabled children? We would have stopped our request if the health, disability, or childhood professionals had advised against this project. This waiting period is also difficult for our children. Each time they see us leave, they ask us if we're going to look for the baby."

I insisted on the spot that we'd considered bringing this child into our life for seven years. I explained to what extent we had been involved in receiving her and how many times we had questioned ourselves during that time. How could our dream be presented "as a goal to be attained, which is unchangeable and never questioned"?

How could it be written that we were disconnected from daily life even though we had six young children?

During our presentation, Philippine remained

undaunted. It even seemed unrealistic at her age (4) to remain so calm and serene while facing a large audience and the solemnity of the situation. What happened in her little head that day? We would never know. But what was certain is that she must have perceived to what extent it was important to us. She understood that, at that moment, we were not playing.

In leaving, we were calm but very weary and empty. It seemed to us that we were running around in circles and endlessly repeating the same statements, and that these statements were wrong each time. We did not have any conclusions about what we said. We did not want to make any more predictions. We had suffered too much every time. We walked lifelessly back to the car. We had given all that we could for two years, and we could no longer do it.

Luckily, daily life was a lifeline. It was important not to allow suffering to invade all our thoughts. We were lucky to be together. We were going to find the children in school. What a joy it was to have them, and how lucky we were to have welcomed them without having to meet any psychiatrists. Midwives are a lot less complicated!

The Stork Would Soon Pass By
December 24

The luggage was checked in. Any minute now, we were waiting for the plane's takeoff. It was supposed to take us to Morocco to celebrate Christmas near Nicolas' aunt, who was in pretty bad shape.

For two days, we were completely stunned. We had learned that the General Council gave us the approval allowing us to welcome you.

I'd never had as many emotions as when I opened the registered letter. The ground seemed to shrink under my feet.

We so badly wanted this "YES" that I was afraid of misreading the letter. So, I called Nicolas. The sentence was unambiguous. I didn't have the time to read everything.

Nicolas' voice got lost in his tears on the phone. He yelled at me between every sob: "It's a yes, it's a yes. We've won!"

I was trembling and crying. The telephone handsets were no longer making any sounds. We could only hear sniffling and spasms. We were unable to talk any longer.

The pressure finally dropped after two years.

December 21, 2012, was not the end of the world, no matter what the Mayans predicted. For us, it was the start of a new life. We did not yet know what the coming days had in store for us, but we knew that the uncertainty had ended. From this moment on, being supported by the adoption agency, we were going to move ahead with the professionals, hand in hand.

We would no longer need to justify the past. We would simply have to keep our eyes fixed on the present and our future — on your future.

I left the post office after crying. I could no longer keep this big news to myself. Who would I call? Who would I start with? The list was long. Reality caught up with me. It was 10:45 a.m. I had to be at school at 11:20 a.m. My tears returned. What a joy it was to be able to announce this news to the children! I looked forward to telling them that we would soon welcome you. But this announcement had to be memorable. Quickly, quickly, I thought. I don't have a lot of time. I headed off to the first corner supermarket. I grabbed some Champomy (sparkling cider), some other drinks, and everything we never bought that would make this day unforgettable. We had to party right away! I was so stunned that I was afraid of forgetting Brune in my rush. She was still so little. I wasn't supposed to neglect her. I stopped to give her a big hug. My tears flowed onto her still chubby neck. I told her that she was going to become a big sister now. My voice must have been convincing. She must have perceived my great joy, because she seemed proud of this announcement even if she surely did not understand everything.

The preceding days had been very difficult. The tension

at home was palpable. Everyone appeared to have suffered from this waiting period that seemed unjustified.

One day, I found Côme crying in the garage, out of sight. He had asked me a few minutes earlier, coming back from school, if we had gotten a response for you. He was inconsolable and said, "But why, Mommy? Tell me why they don't want it." I was powerless. I could not give him an answer. My only answer was to take him in my arms and cry with him.

How could we blithely celebrate Christmas while you were going to be alone?

The news spread like a trail of gunpowder in the school's parking lot. There was a horn "concert." All the people who had arrived there quickly parked to get out of their cars as soon as possible. We gave each other big hugs, cried, laughed, and jumped. It was snowing hard. The scenery's beauty made this moment even more magical. I will always recall this.

This was the victory of an entire village. The teachers were also very moved, and the children, of course, screamed with joy. They expressed the end of this waiting period with their own character and sensitivity. Côme burst into tears of joy and let all the pressure that had accumulated for such a long time come out. Baudouin, who was more reserved, managed to hold back his tears, but we could see them welling up at the corners of his eyes. He stood up straight as a soldier who has won a splendid victory. Tiphaine leaped like a grasshopper. Mockingly, Marin was smiling to see those who were crying. Philou expressed her enthusiasm in song and already claimed that she would sleep with you.

We were looking forward to the end of the day so we could all be together to enjoy and talk about this great news that was going to transform our lives. This day was such a whirlwind! Nicolas could not work. He spent the day buying vintage champagne bottles and dropped them off at the homes of all the people who had helped us so much. A few days before December 25, he perfectly fulfilled his role as

Santa Claus! Time had stopped for him. Nothing was without value in the face of this new life that was entrusted to us. He also called all his close friends, especially Vincent, a longtime companion who witnessed our marriage and our long path toward you. They cried together on the telephone, and, after a while, Nicolas burst out laughing. In the midst of his tears, Vincent declared: "To think that you're crying for joy now, whereas you're going to be stuck with her for the next 60 years!" Yes, this in fact seemed crazy but, once again, the joy of your arrival prevailed over your disability. This sentence would not change. It was another proof that we were well grounded in reality.

Third Chosen Step: Marin

"Yes, Marin, I am crying." Marin, who was embarrassed and amused, tapped his sister on the elbow and discreetly said, "Look, Mommy's crying." He laughed at the same time.

Yes, Marin, I was crying for joy. I was going to be a mommy again. We also cried at the announcement of each pregnancy and on the day of your birth, Côme, Baudouin, Tiphaine, Marin, Philippine, and Brune.

"And Daddy, also?" Oh, yes! I will always remember the amazed look of this little boy discovering that his father, who was so strong and so "everything" for him, could cry with joy.

Yes, this was a powerful moment. It provided the opportunity for us to tell each other how much we meant to each other.

The following day, it was impossible for me to walk because this announcement unnerved me so much. The children were not there for the weekend. For a whole day, I was reveling in this news. Time had come to a halt. I was taking advantage of it and enjoying it. I was sitting cross-legged at the edge of a warming fireplace. My hands were encircling a cup of boiling water, as if to numb them, since

I was dreaming so much of holding you close to me. It was good to be able to dream, at last.

Tears of Joy Gave Way to Tears of Mourning
December 24

After these tears of joy, our hearts were swollen with this promise of love to come. We landed in Rabat on December 24. When we arrived in Nicolas' family home, there was an entirely different atmosphere. In the morning, Mamix, Nicolas' aunt, was unconscious, and her language was incoherent. We understood that the following days would be her last ones on this earth. We learned, through the people who surrounded her, that she had meticulously prepared for our arrival. Everything was lovingly thought of, down to the last detail. For several weeks, everyone was getting agitated to prepare the crèche, fill the fridge, order the turkeys, and buy boxes of chocolate. Little gifts were found in the *souk* [market] that were in accordance with everyone's personality. Everything was ready for us to have great holidays with our family. She let go as soon as we arrived. It was, undoubtedly, not a coincidence. She was waiting for us.

As soon as Nicolas saw the condition his aunt was in, without waiting, he provided all the care she'd need so that she'd suffer as little as possible. He notified the medical staff that was following her. We also decided to prolong our stay to be near her as long as we could.

These two weeks were filled with a lot of emotion. We stayed close to her as much as possible during the day. The children came by. The youngest ones came over to talk to her as if everything was normal. We loved her so much!

She knew all the children inside and out and had fun giving them a nickname, according to their character. She spent a lot of time with them in Évian in the summer or in Morocco in the winter. There, she would give them riddles about the famous "Monsieur *pas-de-i-gare aux gages*"

(Mr. no "i", or there's a penalty), who went to the market. Ah, what memories! There were fun games, long evenings around a good fire, and a cup of *merdadouche* (tea made with dry herbs found in Morocco), when she told me about her family origins. She also talked about long trips in a camping car when she traveled across Spain to return to France. She spoke of the great friendships she made with the poor people to whom she opened her door and heart, and the Romanian and Polish political refugees who crossed the Iron Curtain during the time of the former USSR.

Her room overlooked a landing where we took our naps. We heard her moaning, sighing, and babbling incoherently. It was painful. But we were happy to be able to be with her in order to surround her for her big trip into the afterlife. Luckily, Fabrice, Nicolas' very close brother, arrived as soon as possible. His efficiency and legendary humor allowed us to experience less tragic moments.

Mamix's friends came by, dined with us, and told us about their memories. We experienced some incredible heart-to-heart moments. But our heart was ready to implode. It was caught in a vice between two gigantic emotions. These were your imminent arrival and the departure of the one who was dear to us. We felt, in a very perceptible way, that life and death were intimately connected.

On the morning of December 28, I discovered Mamix's lifeless body. Nicolas and his brother had left to go shopping. It was up to me to tell them about her death. Then, everything was in a whirlwind. What is earthly makes reality heavier. We had to call the funeral home, close her eyes, position her body before it became stiff, choose her clothes in order to give her dignity back to her for her last trip, go through her directory, page by page, to inform her family, prepare her farewell Mass in Morocco, and return her body to Évian so that she would be buried in the family vault.

Her last breath was on the Feast of the Holy Innocents. This echoed your imminent arrival.

WILL YOU
REALLY
ARRIVE?

The Approval in Our Pocket and Later?

February

Days, weeks, and months went by. And there was still no date to meet you. I was very despondent.

I gathered my strength to continue this long letter, for I had to share everything. Our story had not always been easy, and I wanted it to be useful to those who would come after us. In addition to a personal testimony about our adventure, I thought of the weaknesses of the society in which we're living, the one that we'll leave for our children. These have to do with adoption, of course, but also the value of human life from its beginning to its end, the reception given to people who are different, and projects in life that don't follow the norm.

Having received our approval in December, we weren't summoned until February. We found ourselves face-to-face again with the social worker and psychologist duo for a "guessing game."

"Do you know why you are here?" I timidly asked them if it was to talk about a child who was waiting for a family. Ah no, not at all. What an amazing way to start. We asked them to indicate the purpose of our coming.

For the time being, it was not yet out of order to talk about you. For three hours, we had to explain our process again. We answered a barrage of questions, which were sometimes brutal for us. The psychologist harshly asked me, "Will you now tell us what you're expecting from this child?" This question seemed cruel to me. How could we imagine looking for something in a child? This was a child who was, moreover, abandoned and sick. I kept calm and tried to set my feelings aside. I simply responded, "I'm not expecting anything from this child. I just want to love it as much as I can."

No, I wasn't expecting anything from you. I did not show you a way that you had to follow to live up to my expectations. I also did not expect anything from my other children. For me, maternal love is unconditional. But we were operating in a profit-minded society in which we expect something in return for everything that we do.

A few minutes later, she vehemently asked me, "But NOTHING frightens you, Mrs. Noël? Tell me, NOTH- ING?" I nodded my head. "Uh, yes, nothing scares me." I could even have added, "Nothing and nobody will make me renounce what I believe."

At the end of the discussion, there was a complete blur. These two women were telling us that they still needed time to get to know us. We gave them this time, even though we did not understand the usefulness of these two years that were spent in interviews to get our approval.

On Monday, there was a meeting. On Tuesday, there was a meeting. And on Friday? There was a meeting!

With Some "Ifs," We Would Put You in a Bottle
March 1

After having left us for a few weeks without any news, they came to us in our home, in the children's absence. It was then a matter of "redefining the vision of the Down syndrome child who could be ours."

They explained their fears. They were afraid that we had an idea about Down syndrome that was too naïve. They admitted that a little girl was waiting in their wards. They had anticipated talking about it during their visit, but the doctor was worried about the condition of her health. It seemed that she was autistic. This information was catastrophic for them, whereas it gave us peace of mind. We had, in fact, prepared for the "worst," knowing that Down syndrome has varying degrees of impairment. The association that was supporting us had always frankly warned us. They never tried to obscure reality. They never told us that this would be easy.

In the face of our calmness, they clearly imagined that we were living in a world that was disconnected from reality. So, after the first interview's guessing game, they started another one, the game about "ifs" and "nevers." You'd think we were in a Pierre Palmade (a French actor) skit. But what "if" she "never" loved you, what if she "never" looked at you, etc.

After a few minutes, we only heard "ifs" and "nevers" that were jostling around in our heads. And why should we "never" trust the future or in the power of Love? How would you master your future if you were only 4 months old? And "if" we gave you a chance, what chance? And even "if" you were autistic, or even "if" you "never" looked at us, even "if"... even "if"...why would you not have the right to have a family that loves you — one that was without the conditional "if" or the exclusive "never"? And "if ever" you were simply a human being?

For us, the trouble of consulting was clear. We already talked about it. We were taking you! It didn't matter "if" you were more or less battered. We were taking you! There was no need for a perfect karyotype. We weren't a recruitment agency. We were only parents! And that seemed evident to us — from a neutral and impersonal "he," we had arrived at a "she." It was she. It was you, as you were. Period!

But that did not satisfy them. The social worker and the psychologist thought it would impose too heavy of a burden on us. So, they suggested that we abandon everything. Finally, they were even embarrassed to offer us a Down syndrome child who was "not normal." Ah, this "tyranny of normality," the scourge of our society. Do we all think that we are normal? Who is normal? We obviously are not normal, but then ... not at all!

We were ready to sign a release for them. They suggested a meeting with a psychiatrist.

A Little Meeting ... A Big Step Toward You
March 22

The meeting with the psychiatrist started off tensely. This was the case each time, but we did not get used to it.

She spoke by herself for one hour, explaining adoption in general to us. We patiently listened to her. We then more precisely addressed the situation of all those abandoned and sick children, the ones who are called "special ones" — those whom families did not expect. Nicolas is very sensitive about this subject. He was quite moved, and that was obvious. His eyes became more and more cloudy. She stopped abruptly and shared her astonishment with us. "Mister Noël" had been described to her as a cold person who was aloof about this project. She saw that he had an "enormous, sensitive heart." Those were her words.

The atmosphere lightened up, and the conversation took a different turn. She explained that she did not understand, in seeing us now, how our candidacy could have been the object of so much controversy. She accepted our request and offered to write a letter attesting to our perfect knowledge of this little ward's health condition. She promised that we would go to the Family Council the following month and that she would now do all she could to ensure that things would go fast.

But, our patience was tested further when we learned that no Family Council was planned in April. We would have to wait until May.

The Telephone Call
Friday, May 17

The news finally broke! And I weighed my words. She was not arriving. She was "coming down" on us and made us lose our footing.

We were together on Friday, May 17, 2013, at 6 p.m. When I heard, on the other end of the handset, "Hello! Mrs. Noël?" I immediately understood that it was the tutor. I gasped for air and responded with a muffled "yes." She told us that we were now the parents of a little Marie, who was 6 months old. This woman was extremely jovial. She expressed her joy and warmly thanked me. In her whole career, this was the second time that she would place a Down syndrome child in an adoptive family. She spoke to me with a lot of feeling about her meeting with the first family, who also had several natural children. It was a great blessing for her. She did not understand why our case was the subject of so much controversy. We were the only applicant family. Her choice did not take long. This woman explained that they always had more disabled children than willing families. It was the other way around for children without special needs.

She did not give me any details on your history. We had a meeting on the following Monday at 9 a.m.

The end of the conversation was not very clear to me. I was already somewhere else. I do not know if I even said "Goodbye, Ma'am" or "Sir." I simply said "Thank you, thank you … thank you," over and over again.

We had no more tears or voice. We stayed next to each other and were completely drunk with this news. I felt exactly the same as when I was pregnant. Words are not strong enough to express what we felt. We remained silent, for fear of ruining this moment. Our happiness was so powerful that we no longer knew if we were in a dream or in reality. For fear of shattering this dream, just in case, we reveled in it. It was completely crazy. We slowly understood that the meeting was approaching. I was really excited. I was looking forward to it so much.

Finally, Your Story
May 21

The following Monday, we met the tutor to hear your story and the reasons for your abandonment. It was difficult. We suffered so much for you. Your parents had desired and loved you for nine months. You had a peaceful and loving life *in utero.* This was sweet for me to hear. When you were born, the doctors discovered your illness. Your parents did not feel able to bring you up. They gave you life, Marie. Without them, you would not be here, and we would never have been able to meet you.

The tutor asked us if we wanted to change your first name. No. We would also call you MARIE, the anagram of AIMER (to love). We had discussed it for a long time and jointly decided to keep your first name in any event. If you had come from another ethnic group, that would have reflected your origins and history. We wanted to build upon what you had already experienced, not deny it. We did not want to shape you according to our desires, and that started with respect for your first name. Whatever it was, it was the final imprint of your biological mother, the one who carried you and gave you life. This was our choice.

And besides that, you would have already experienced so many changes when you arrived in our home. We wanted to leave you your only point of reference, which was this first name that you had heard since your birth. It was a little two-syllable word that you could rely on. It was an unchangeable little nothing that was so important. It was your identity.

A Date That Is Tattooed on Our Hearts
May 24 at 2 p.m.

Today, I at last had this little piece of life that was fragile and strong at the same time, in my arms! Marie, you were so calm. Your big blue eyes went deep into ours. We had the sensation that you were probing our hearts. Did you think we were capable? Your opinion was more important for us than those of all the specialists. We felt so small. The suffering of your abandonment, mixed with your disability, was like a mirror reflecting on us. Nicolas was crying. The emotion was so strong. You looked at him with eyes that were full of love and were attracted to him as if you already knew him. It was incredible. There you were, together for life. You seemed to be telling him, "I was waiting for you."

The emotion was very strong for me also. What an unforgettable moment. You curled up in my arms and looked good and so peaceful. I felt alive. In the midst of our tears, we burst out laughing. You were so beautiful! We had prepared ourselves for everything during this long path. And here we were with the prettiest baby it was possible to see in our arms. Your features were thin. You were a perfect little doll. You still had very little hair, minuscule ears, magnificent almond blue eyes, and a tiny bit of a nose that seemed impossible to blow! Your skin was completely soft. You were a magnificent "Cadum" (a brand of French soap) baby. You were 6 months old, but were like a little "flea" that seemed as if it was 3 months old.

For a week, we went to see you every day in the children's home. This time was mandatory to get to know you. We dreamed about walking away with you, because it was obvious that we already knew you and felt that you also knew us. The merger took place immediately, which was natural. But, once again, for the last time, we had to be patient. We could not jump the gun. You really deserved that!

Everyone who took care of you was adorable. It was very comforting for us to see how loved you were. This marvelous team welcomed us quite warmly. They were happy to see Marie settle down with a family. Marie was the only Down syndrome child in this children's home. They told us how painful it was to see the others leave, whereas Marie had never been chosen. The person in charge of the children's home was brimming with warmth and humanity. Marie's primary caregiver also meant a lot to us. A magnificent album was put together, of photos taken since her birth. It included some very touching commentaries. We are keeping it safe and sound and are eager to present it to you when you are old enough to understand. These encounters were part of the most beautiful moments of our lives.

Nicolas, who was very busy professionally, had to cut his visit short one day. I was alone. You were particularly agitated that day. I held you tight, and I calmly said in your ear, "It's over with ... really over with. We are here for good, Marie. I love you as you are. You don't have to put any pressure on yourself. We will never abandon you." My tears were flowing like a river. I had told you, and I will repeat it as much as needed that yes, I love you as you are, from the outset.

You reacted very strongly, grumbled, and then, suddenly, after a long sigh, your head weighed down on my shoulder, and you went to sleep. I heard your steady and serene breathing. You seemed to have become confident. My shoulder will be solid for you, Marie, and we will lead you to your happiness.

The children each came, in turn, to see you, their little sister. They've "taken you in" with incredible ease.

Baudouin admitted his apprehension, but decreed when he saw you, "It's like clockwork. She is so beautiful!"

Marin, in taking you in his arms, saw your smile and declared, "Marie, that's it. YOU adopted me. I'm your brother. My name is Marin!"

They were all very touching and protective towards you.

They "fought" each other to carry you. They all dreamed of only one thing, which was that you be at home with them.

In Your Nest ... For Life
May 31

The big day arrived. On May 31, 2013, the car was really full. Now, you took your place in Brune's Maxi-Cosi car seat. She had really grown. She had only been a 2-month-old infant at the beginning of our adventure, and she was already 2 years old!

It was the usual excitement at home. Your bed had been ready since the beginning of January. We had chosen your cuddly toys, your baby sleeping bag, etc. Everyone wanted to sleep with you, and we, especially, did not know if they would be able to let you sleep. Brune would feel lucky to share her room. She, who was usually so capricious, was completely calm and so proud.

The first night was magical. It was impossible for me to sleep. I stayed seated on a little chair that stuck to your bed. I held your hand, which was so small. You slept peacefully, as if you had always been settled in your "nest." I didn't get tired of seeing you suck your little index finger, with the palm of your hand pointing to the sky. I looked at you like a treasure, a treasure that was finally found.

A Very Nice Medical Meeting
June

Marie, you were a ward of the state, who was born in Paris. Since your abandonment, you had been followed every month by the Jérôme Lejeune Foundation's consultancy. This doctor had dedicated his life to medical research on genetic illnesses of the mind. He also wanted to welcome and care for people — children and adults — who were suffering from Down syndrome. Jérôme Lejeune worked for the defense of life and respect for the patient's dignity with an ongoing concern for ethics and an active solidarity from the beginning of life to death.

A meeting was scheduled for June. Naturally, we decided to honor it. It was extremely interesting for us to meet a doctor who was known to be experienced.

The doctor who had followed you since birth warmly welcomed us. He was careful to talk with each of the children, explaining to them why they were here today. He asked a few questions about our family and our path. Not for a moment did he praise me with compliments about the fact that we had adopted you. That was ideal, for I would not have wanted to hear that talk. I came to this meeting to have as much information as possible in order to help you grow up. I felt confident with this man, and I liked his way of doing his job with such kindness and intelligence.

This meeting was very important for us. It informed us about the condition of your health and your mental state. We were able to get some information from those who were concerned on what they observed about you, and about how you had evolved during these first seven months of life and the care that had to be given to you.

We got a lot of advice. What a joy it was to be able to approach specialists who looked at human beings so kindly, whoever they were. This was part of the wonderful meetings that moved us forward in life.

I was extremely sensitive to the conclusions they gave me after having examined you. He was very moved to see you like this. The doctor thought you had already changed a lot. He even said your behavior was very different. He had the impression of facing another little girl. He explained that during these last meetings, you were "a small bar of soap in one's arms." It was not possible to make eye contact with you. He was very worried, assuming that you had perhaps had some convulsions. During this interview, you were totally calm and completely nestled in my arms. I carried you like a kangaroo because I came in the subway. You devoured me with your eyes. Our relationship was totally natural for me. You were my daughter! I understood that the magic of love was already working by not wasting any time. You had only been home for a week.

Prelude to a New Life

August 6

We were in Évian. It was 5:30 p.m. The rain had been falling ruthlessly since this morning. A little clearing seemed to appear in the midst of this threatening weather. I put on my sneakers. The children watched an episode of "Zorro." They were being supervised by the marvelous Quitterie, the young girl who was keeping an eye on them. Marie was sleeping like an angel.

I plugged in my headphones, cranked up the music, and ran down the steps of the terrace, four at a time. I had the impression of being 14, and that was fitting since we were going to celebrate our 14 years of marriage in a few days. Our marriage was a starting point in my life and a mutual commitment that allowed us to experience this great joy today.

I ran along Lake Geneva. The sky was gray. I hardly saw Switzerland at the other end of the stretch of water. The lake seemed to be infinite. My heart swelled. Love is also infinite. What a joy!

I ran while screaming these words: "To love to the point of losing your mind. To love to the point of not knowing what to do with it."

After 45 minutes of running time, I found a deserted beach. I bathed under the rain, which had come back with a vengeance. What a joy!

It had been more than four months since I had jumped into my sneakers. The last meetings had exhausted us so much that I didn't have enough energy.

After a nice hot shower and a steaming cup of tea, with my hair still wet, I picked up my pen again. The end of it was almost dry. It was a long time since it had touched my notebook.

We had you close to us, Marie. We were finally all together.

You woke up to your own rhythm. You thumbed your nose at the scholarly books that described a baby's usual evolution. You were 9 months old, had no teeth, were not being spoon-fed, were not yet holding your head up well, and couldn't sit up at all. But your gaze was more intense than ever. It touched our hearts. You hugged like no one else.

You taught us to live by breaking rules. We understood, thanks to you, that you have to take life as it comes, with patience and love, without which life escapes us.

You forced us to stop several hours a day in the whirlwind of our existence, for everything took longer with you. The meals lasted a long time. You did not drink easily. It was impossible to put a baby bottle in your mouth that had a teddy bear's paw on it! You looked at us while nursing, and you, our little "weasel," made us aware of what life is about. There was no need to read all the philosophies or to run everywhere for answers. Happiness was here. It was quite close and simple.

You also taught us to contemplate and revel in simple things, which were so simple that, in general, we did not see them. But it was so good to find them again. We have to let go.

The long nightmare had given way to this sweet dream. We were all floating in happiness and high on this new life that had just been added to our family.

The children spent all their time with you. We were impressed by this merger. Yes, your addition was succeeding. It was succeeding even faster than we could have imagined. You were pampered like a princess. Your brothers and sisters were touched by your least gestures, expressions, and funny faces. Every morning, they raced to see you wake up and stretch. It was magical. They played with you without getting tired. You never stayed alone in your playpen for long. One came to play, and another one went by and gave you a kiss on your hair. Another one sang you some songs, while yet another one cuddled up and stretched out against you, while sniffing your little baby smell. You had become everyone's cuddly toy and our family's mascot. They proudly introduced you to their friends. They argued so much to have you that they unanimously said, "We must have a Marie for everyone!" All of them, in their own way, seemed to be saying, "I was expecting you."

Nicolas was keeping the baby bottle for himself at night. He could, in this way, take advantage of talking to you. Even if he came home late, he absolutely wanted to keep this moment to be alone with you. Each time, it was a very moving tête-à-tête. After you finished your bottle, he stayed to talk with you for a long time. Your big blue eyes met his, and all seemed to disappear around you. Nothing else existed. It was fascinating. I delighted in all these moments.

The joy was very intense for me. I cherished you while the group was in school. Otherwise, it was impossible to get near you! I spent hours looking at you, talking to you, dancing with you, and holding you tight, very tight in my arms. Your gaze was so intense that you seemed to be saying thank you to me each time. It was as if we already knew each other and had found each other again after a long absence. Yes, I was waiting for you. My tears of joy were very often flowing onto your hair. When you felt that I was crying, your breathing was different. It was faster and was rising. Our hearts understood each other. We had each really suffered from our separation. I did not completely manage to figure out that we had arrived at the end of this long journey. There were such ups and downs required to get to you!

This book was closing while our life's new pages were being written.

Yes, it was closing where everything was starting. We had finally gotten to you! Our goal was not to possess you, but to love you. We could look at you sleeping, hold you tight in our arms when you were suffering, and help you wake up.

It was not the end of a story, but, on the contrary, a point of departure. We were going to try to reach out with all our might to the verb "to love" and to conjugate it in the present tense every day of our lives. There would certainly be difficult moments. We have our limits, and our patience sometimes wears thin.

We would keep fighting, but in a different way. It would no longer be about an administrative path strewn with pit-falls, but another fight against ourselves. It would be a battle as a couple, whose stake would be our ability to question ourselves so we could accept our mistakes and move forward — especially, our ability to remain humble in front of you and the great joy that you offered us.

An Endless Song!

Our home consisted, primarily, of endless card games on the rug, interminable Monopoly sessions where we were always dreaming of buying the rue de la Paix, buddies who dropped by unannounced, dinners where we remade the world until the early morning, the lice removal evenings, the freezer that was full of hairbrushes to kill lice, the laundry basket that was still full, unmatched socks, toys in all the corners, the conniving bursts of laughter when the youngest child said "thank you" after having burped, the shouts, the tantrums, the monstrous pieces of luggage, the mended cuddly toys that were forgotten in an interstate rest area, the bread and jam that always fell upside down, the sleeve in the gravy, the sticky fingers on the touchscreen tablet, the crumbs in the bed, the alarm clock failures, the first steps, the smiles with two teeth, the fingernail polish that never dried, the closet full of little messes, the noodle necklaces, the multiplication tables, and the eternal exceptions: choux, hiboux, genoux, cailloux, joujoux — another eux! (cabbages, owls, knees, pebbles, toys). Because of all these good things, we were surely not going to stop there!

And like the song of the "three little cats" (a French song) that we all had in mind or the story of Father Castor's big black panther, we didn't want any of that to ever stop, but to go on and on. So, we started again:

"The endless card games on the rug, the interminable Monopoly sessions where we were always dreaming of buying the rue de la Paix ..."

And Philou kept singing this song: "Don't be sad, Marie. Up there, in Heaven, you'll no longer have Down syndrome."

AFTERWORD

This diary of a mother can be read in many ways. First, as the testimony of a couple on its path to adopt a disabled child. It is a story that might help other parents who might be tempted to do the same. You can also see a plea in favor of human life in it, especially when it's been wounded in the very beginning. Loving life, in fact, is not to take advantage, in a selfish way, of the physical and moral goods that we have received. It's to protect the lives of others. In these pages, you can also find a treatise on spirituality that is full of biblical references. This includes the call to leave your country, the fruit of your womb, the father who loses his voice during his child's gestation, and the numerous references to Psalm verses. This spiritual ascension of a couple and their children conjures up Élisabeth Leseur's famous remark: *"Everyone who rises lifts the world up."*

My gaze is that of the pediatrician who was privileged to follow Marie since her first weeks of life, thanks to the confidence of the team from the children's home where she stayed, and then to see her again after her arrival in her adoptive family.

From the very beginning of her life, Marie was confronted with two difficulties. The first one was this extra chromosome 21, which defines Down syndrome. The second difficulty, which flows from the preceding one, was that her biological parents had not wanted to think of her as "the flesh of their flesh."

We must really understand that the situation of the child who is entrusted by its biological parents with being adopted is not always the same in every case, depending on the reasons which pushed these parents to make such a decision.

In fact, at best, it's about a young, very impoverished woman, who has no professional activity and no family support. She understands that she will not have the material and moral means to bring this child up. But she loves this child and lovingly entrusts it, hoping that it will find parents who will give it all that it will need. Therefore, this child has been carried during its pregnancy, and also at the moments of its birth, by a lot of maternal love.

In the case of abandonment for a chromosomal disorder or another anomaly that is visible at birth, the discovery of the disability is associated with an intense trauma. This is true both for the biological parents and for the child who is often present when the disability is announced. This child is overwhelmed by the parents' rejection. We must not misunderstand the importance of this wound that can impede the child's good mental development.

Marie's story, which is far from being finished since she is still only a baby, started like a fairy tale. From the beginning of her life, Marie knew how to touch the professionals who took care of her in the maternity ward of the child welfare services agency and the children's home. These professionals came together in an important way and implemented all the means that were at their disposal to improve her situation.

In fact, very early on, her psychomotor and relational development appeared to be much worse than what is normally observed in a Down syndrome infant of the same age. She was a baby who had severe hypotonia, a dwindling mobility, bad breastfeeding, and feeble responsiveness. Such a picture could evoke a severe neurological impairment, but also a state of mental distress. After having been assured of the normality of the cerebral imagery, the electroencephalogram, heart, and thyroid gland, the hypothesis of a state of great mental suffering was retained. The team in the children's home decided to take it on in the most intense way possible.

This team, therefore, accentuated the carrying and feeding care, recruited a psychomotor therapist and, in collaboration with the social services department, looked for a foster care placement that would allow these measures to be intensified even more. Thanks to this mobilization, we noted the child's true mental reanimation. She opened herself up to relationships, started to eat better, and improved her energy as well as her motor skills function. Then, there was some happy news. A family was an applicant for her adoption.

As I'm writing these lines, everything is going well. Marie is progressing "in strength and wisdom." Her brothers, sisters, and parents, as well as her extended family and entourage, are happy. Joy is filling the home.

In his *Technical and Critical Vocabulary of Philosophy* (Editions PUF, 1926, 2010, Paris), André Lalande recalls that the first meaning of "family," or *familia* in Latin, refers to all the servants. This meaning really applies to little Marie's story. The family consists of the people who are at the child's service.

In the very young child, psychological care first requires bodily care (washing up, a baby bottle, being carried, and strokes), which allow for skin-to-skin contact, the exchange of odors, looks, and mimicking — all of it supported by a lot of words.

The one who ensures a child's development is a parent. The final dialogue of Marcel Pagnol's play *Fanny* has to do with knowing who little Césariot's father is. Is it Marius, the biological father, who abandoned Fanny to cross the sea, or Panisse, who married her and took care of the baby? This scene has remained in everyone's memory:

"But, finally, you know very well that the child is my son."

"Of course, I know it. They look like two peas

in a pod. But, nonetheless, he [Honoré] is kind of his father. When this child was born, he weighed four kilos, which were created by his mother. He's now up to seven kilos. ... These additional kilos are three kilos of love. I gave my fair share. ... His mother, naturally, has given a lot. But Honoré is the one who has given the most. And what have you given him? Life. Dogs also give life. Nonetheless, they are not fathers... And then, you didn't want this child. Don't say that you gave him life. He took it from you." (Marcel Pagnol, *Fanny*, Éditions de Fallois, 2004, Paris).

We must pay tribute to all the teams of social workers who evaluate prospective adoptive parents. Their work is all the more important if it's about a very fragile disabled child. I've had the great sorrow, during my career, of knowing dramatic situations where special needs children had been abandoned a few months after their adoption by adoptive parents who thought the task was too heavy or others who found themselves to be victims of abuse.

Angelism (which claims that humans are basically angelic) is a trap into which militant couples can fall. This risk is very astutely suggested in this book when the author writes that she and her husband were not "seated on a soft cloud where every bird sang the Angelus."

I would be tempted to conclude, at the risk of seeming to play with words, that, to really welcome an abandoned child, a total and wholehearted act of abandonment into love and truth is required. May Marie and her family have a long and happy life!

Dr. Aimé Ravel
Pediatrician Qualified in Medical Genetics
Consulting Manager
of the Jérôme Lejeune Institute

ACKNOWLEDGMENTS

Thanks to Nicolas, who bore my tirades when facing misunderstandings and who supported my imagination every day.

Thanks to Tim and Martine for their magnificent preface.

Thanks to Dr. Aimé Ravel for his immense support, proofreading, and wonderful afterword.

Thanks to Carine, my "alter ego," who has listened to me for eight years. She's the first close friend who resonated so much with us. Thanks for the exhilarating afternoons when we were lucky to remake the world!

Thanks to Stéph for all the Coke breaks, such great times, the texts — the one who discovered the secret without a clue ... over the top!

Thanks to Margot, Ghislain, Anne-Laure, the very efficient godfathers and godmothers, who were always there. Ah ... the nights spent chatting in Évian ... what will be left: "Nico? It's my life!"

Thanks to Jo and Stéphanie for all their wisdom and great faith...

Thanks to Béné, my little creative trend finder, my neon touch, her pep, and her collusion with Charlie!

Thanks to Marguerite for her philosophical touch!

Thanks to Christelle for her great sensitivity, friendship, and to Valoche, with the flaming hair, who will make Marie's next dresses, which will be inspired by the Dior/Chanel collections.

Thanks to my Paulette for having corrected and typed my manuscript with agile fingers and for all the fun times since the harvest! And, in particular, her '70s carpet!

Thanks to Vinc' for his proofreading, support, listening, help, and tears.

Thanks to Antoine, Marieka, and Grégoire ... Marie's fan club!

Thanks to Sophie for her support and great drive to want to do things differently in order to move things forward.

Thanks to all the fairies — Henriette, Clem, Lolo, Doro, Nathalie, Ln, Marie, Cynthia, Marie-Agnès, Isabelle, Cécile, Marie-Anne, Marie-Amélie, Marieka, Iza, Mélanie, Sandra, Caroline, Océane, Amélie, Anne-Lise, Claire-Lise, Aurélie, Karine, Gaëlle.

Thanks to Virginie, my favorite graphic artist, for her help, which was so effective, and her expertise.

Thanks to Bernard, our crazy creator, for his help and, in particular, his ability to give you a shot in the arm.

Thanks to FX for his web help!

And, of course, THANKS to Grégoire for all his work and his folly for having, without knowing us, embarked on this adventure. Without him, nothing would have been possible.

Thanks to Alix for his college friendship.

Thanks to Cécile, Jacquot, Sabine, and Marco for the great pizza parties and for listening to all our stories...

Thanks to Lolotte for the evenings on public park benches and for the personal coaching to help face the world!

Thanks to PA and Charlotte for their efficient help in moving on to the editing.

Thanks to Anne-Jo, Bert, and Pascal for having embarked, in such a moving way, on our madness. Thanks for being so close to us!

Thanks to Blan, Claire, and Pat for their great friendship!

Thanks to Uncle Dominique and Béné for their kindness and medical point of view.

Thanks to Raph for his help and to Marie for the times that we talked.

Thanks to Mme Pipou for her precious proofreading.

Thanks to Mme Haen for her pretty home by the sea, a magnificent place where I was able to finish writing this book.

Thanks to Maylis, my dear friend, who beat us to the afterlife. She's still at my side day and night. She taught me to live without being afraid.

She's the one who so kindly called me Mary Poppins.

Tombée du Nid (Fallen from the Nest) Association

Association Tombée du Nid

4 impasse Germaine
78480 Verneuil-sur-Seine – France

tombeedunid.com

tombeedunid@gmail.com

Dear friends,

Before closing this book, I would like, first of all, to thank you for having shared this adventure with us. But I would especially like you to know that I did not choose to write this book. It was obvious that it had to be written. It was like an urgent call to testify to all that Marie has taught us and given us by opening up her heart.

So, as a family, we decided to assign all the copyrights linked to the sale of this book so that they are fully paid back to the Tombée du Nid association, which we created for the occasion. This book is only the start of a greater adventure.

This association, which was declared under the July 1, 1901 law and the August 16, 1901 decree, is about:

— Helping those who are weak, impoverished, and in difficult situations, regardless of the cause.
— The promotion of mutual assistance and support to those who are the most disadvantaged and of their integration into society.
— The encouragement of solidarity between people in society.
— The fight against exclusion in general.
— The financial and logistical support of initiatives working in this way.

What boat are we getting into? Where will all this lead us?

As Antoine de Saint-Exupéry wrote, "If you want to build a boat, don't gather your men and women together to boss them around, to explain every detail to them, to say something to them, or to find something. ... If you want to build a boat, make the desire of the sea arise in the hearts of your men and women."

Dear friends, if you feel like it, come on board with us! We are counting on you!

– Clotilde

DIVINE MERCY
RESOURCES

Join the
Association of Marian Helpers,
headquartered at the National Shrine of The Divine Mercy, and share in special blessings!

An invitation from Fr. Joseph, MIC, the director

Marian Helpers is an Association of Christian faithful of the Congregation of Marian Fathers of the Immaculate Conception. By becoming a member, you share in the spiritual benefits of the daily Masses, prayers, and good works of the Marian priests and brothers.

This is a special offer of grace given to you by the Church through the Marians. Please consider this opportunity to share in these blessings, along with others whom you would wish to join into this spiritual communion.

The Marian Fathers of the Immaculate Conception of the Blessed Virgin Mary is a religious congregation of nearly 500 priests and brothers around the world.

Call 1-800-462-7426 or visit marian.org

Give a Consoling Gift: *Prayer*

Enroll your loved ones in the Association of Marian Helpers, and they will participate in the graces from the daily Masses, prayers, good works, and merits of the Marian priests and brothers around the world.

Enrollments can be offered for the living or deceased. We offer a variety of enrollment cards: wedding, anniversary, First Holy Communion, birthday, get well, and more.

1-800-462-7426 • marian.org/enrollments

Request a Mass
to be offered by the Marian Fathers for your loved one

Individual Masses
(for the living or deceased)

Gregorian Masses (30 days of consecutive Masses for the deceased)

1-800-462-7426 • marian.org/mass

Visit the National Shrine of The Divine Mercy in Stockbridge, Massachusetts!

The Shrine is a ministry of the Marian Fathers of the Immaculate Conception and offers daily Masses, Confessions, prayers, and more.

For more information, visit TheDivineMercy.org/shrine or call (413) 298-3931.

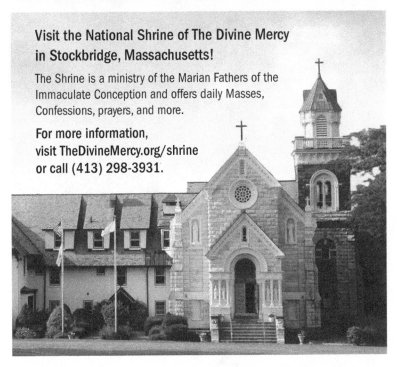